The Virtual Campus
Technology and Reform in Higher Educ[ation]

by Gerald C. Van Dusen

ASHE-ERIC Higher Education Report Volume 25, Number 5

Prepared by

Clearinghouse on Higher Education
The George Washington University

In cooperation with

Association for the Study
of Higher Education

Published by

Graduate School of Education and Human Development
The George Washington University

Jonathan D. Fife, Series Editor

Cite as

Van Dusen, Gerald C. 1997. *The Virtual Campus: Technology and Reform in Higher Education.* ASHE-ERIC Higher Education Report Volume 25, No. 5. Washington, D.C.: The George Washington University, Graduate School of Education and Human Development.

Library of Congress Catalog Card Number 97-73368
ISSN 0884-0040
ISBN 1-878380-77-X

Managing Editor: Lynne J. Scott
Manuscript Editor: Judy A. Beck
Cover Design by Michael David Brown, Inc., The Red Door
   Gallery, Rockport, ME

The ERIC Clearinghouse on Higher Education invites individuals to submit proposals for writing monographs for the *ASHE-ERIC Higher Education Report* series. Proposals must include:
1. A detailed manuscript proposal of not more than five pages.
2. A chapter-by-chapter outline.
3. A 75-word summary to be used by several review committees for the initial screening and rating of each proposal.
4. A vita and a writing sample.

ERIC Clearinghouse on Higher Education
Graduate School of Education and Human Development
The George Washington University
One Dupont Circle, Suite 630
Washington, DC 20036-1183

The mission of the ERIC system is to improve American education by increasing and facilitating the use of educational research and information on practice in the activities of learning, teaching, educational decision making, and research, wherever and whenever these activities take place.

This publication was prepared partially with funding from the Office of Educational Research and Improvement, U.S. Department of Education, under contract no. ED RR-93-002008. The opinions expressed in this report do not necessarily reflect the positions or policies of OERI or the Department.

EXECUTIVE SUMMARY

The *virtual campus* is a metaphor for the electronic teaching, learning, and research environment created by the convergence of powerful new information and instructional technologies. Today there is a pressing call for technology to provide expanded higher education opportunities to a very wide spectrum of present and potential clientele.

What Are the Implications of Teaching on the Virtual Campus?

A paradigmatic shift, from a professor-centered to a student-centered system of learning, has particular implications for the profession of teaching. One implication is a recommitment to creating an ideal learning environment for students, employing new technologies to address variances from the ideal. A second major implication for faculty is a shift from traditional to new roles and classroom responsibilities. The transition from lecturer to facilitator will not happen overnight and must be accompanied by institutional and professional commitment to incorporate research findings into professional development activities. Beyond merely providing technical training in the latest (and soon obsolete) technology, professional development activities will need to focus on crucial classroom variables that will ultimately determine the level of productive interaction and intellectual engagement apropos to the individual and group (Barr and Tagg 1995).

How Will Classroom Learning Be Different?

Systemic reform has brought about a number of changes to postsecondary education, none more significant than what students learn and how they learn it. With time and distance effectively removed as constraints, colleges and universities are serving a more heterogeneous clientele with diverse educational backgrounds and needs. As Plater (1994) suggests, "these new century students confront us with the possibility that a postsecondary educational system designed to manage enrollment growth by weeding out unprepared or uncommitted students may no longer be appropriate or economically defensible" (p. 9).

Perhaps the most telling difference between learning in the traditional and virtual modes is the kind and extent of interaction. In the traditional classroom, the potential for learner-instructor and learner-learner is very high, but instructors have largely ignored this mandate for change and continue to employ the lecture mode as the predominant method of instruction. In the virtual classroom, on the other hand, technology supports collaborative learning, heterogeneous groupings, problem-solving, and higher order thinking skills—educational processes that a lecture format cannot facilitate.

What Will Be the New Scholarly Agenda for Research?

Today's American higher education establishment is an aggregate of three functions—teaching, service, and research. Critics of American higher education today contend that especially since the Second World War faculty have placed emphasis on the research function to the detriment of teaching and service at a time when our culture demands the preparation of workers for a competitive and volatile economy. Voices from within the academy have proposed a reconceptualization of scholarship, one that expands the practice of present-day research to include integration, application, and teaching (Boyer 1990).

New forms of scholarship may necessitate a new epistemology. The scholarships of integration, application, and teaching entail "action" research that may fall outside the boundaries of prevailing institutional epistemology. College and universities must become learning organizations that foster originality and innovation.

Can Technology Help to Create a Culture of Quality?

Calls from external constituencies for academic institutions to demonstrate greater accountability and systemic improvement have prompted many colleges and universities to adopt the principles of Total Quality Management (TQM). Less a set of specific tools than an underlying philosophy, TQM has been distilled by Chaffee and Sherr (1992) into three simple ideas: defining quality in terms of customer needs, bettering work performance, and improving administration. If TQM is the underlying philosophy, Information Resource Management is the facilitator of broad access to information.

In the academic sphere, TQM faces stiff faculty resistance. Many faculty see TQM as "another management fad from the evil empire of business" (Chaffee and Sherr 1992, p. 93). If academic TQM is to emerge as an agent of organizational reform, it is likely to come about more through faculty initiative than external pressure.

How Can the Governance and Finance Considerations Be Managed?

As large sums of money are contemplated and eventually allocated for educational technology development, college and university boards face a number of daunting tasks (Krebs 1996). First, boards must closely monitor regulatory legislation and actively participate in public policy debate. Distance education providers must stay abreast of federal and state regulations, which often adversely affect the interstate delivery of programs and services. Second, boards must establish a telecommunications policy and a strategic plan for its implementation. Third, boards must shepherd resources by defining genuine instructional needs and identifying appropriate technological solutions to fulfill them.

What Conclusions and Recommendations Can Be Drawn?

Colleges and universities are just now crossing the threshold between modest experimentation with and mainstream adoption of information technologies (El-Khawas 1995; Green 1996b). Because of the serious repercussions reform efforts are already having on the academy, a number of conclusions and recommendations are warranted. Following are seven conclusions: (1) a paradigm shift can occur only in institutions committed to comprehensive reform; (2) attempts to change the classroom focus from "the sage on the stage" to collaborative learning are likely to fail without a substantial commitment to professional development; (3) higher education will continue to be market driven, requiring redoubled efforts to define academic productivity; (4) new constituencies appear to be well served by a variety of available distance learning venues; (5) the TQM movement has made impressive inroads in higher education administration; however, very little penetration has occurred where it most matters—on the academic side of the institution; (6) even as instructional use of technology rises, institutional support for applications development has been dilatory; and (7) the historic commitment to core values in traditional undergraduate education has wavered; the same vacillation threatens to undermine general education requirements in electronically delivered certificate and degree programs.

In the absence of conclusive data with respect to wise technology choices and successful teaching/learning models, institutions must carefully prepare today for what is anticipated as a widespread integration of information into teaching, learning, and research. Following are seven recommendations for beginning this process of integration: (1) create a venue where key stakeholders can analyze major technology issues and purchases; (2) assert the value of technology-based learning from a variety of research perspectives; (3) establish quality standards for certificate and degree programs; (4) avoid pitting traditionalists against technology enthusiasts; (5) make *collaboration* and *cooperation,* not *reengineering* and *restructuring,* the new institutional buzz-words; (6) retain a strong commitment to adequate library staffing and funding; and (7) prepare for success by creating the necessary support structures.

CONTENTS

FOREWORD

The use of the word *virtual,* as in the virtual campus, the virtual classroom, or the virtual library, is intended to convey the meaning of the use of electronics in enabling the flow of information for specific reasons. The success in creating a virtual world depends upon how clearly the objective(s) has been defined and to what extent the processes necessary for the accomplishment of the objective have been designed.

For many institutions, the purchase and use of electronic technologies have been done using the Mount Everest mentality. This "because it's there" approach to electronic technology has institutions purchasing the newest and best equipment for fear that if they don't, they will not appear to be an institution that is on the cutting edge. This approach also can be likened to the Yuppie toy approach; i.e., the institution with the most toys wins.

The institution that approaches the virtual campus concept with the attitude that the new technologies are merely better tools that can be used to help the institution effectively and efficiently achieve its educational mission will be far more successful in the long run. Using this approach, institutions will take a holistic approach to the use of technologies. They will ask basic questions such as: What is the long term vision for our institution? What education outcomes are our faculty striving for? What are the skills and support systems necessary to unify the education mission of the institution with faculty performance? What role will the new technologies play in helping all areas of the institution be successful in meeting their responsibilities? Helping us to understand the complexities and interrelationships of the virtual campus is the purpose of this report.

Gerald C. Van Dusen, professor of English with an emphasis in distance education at Wayne County Community College, has reviewed over 200 publications in his effort to synthesize the knowledge base concerning the virtual campus. The author begins by first examining the assumptions underlying teaching in higher education and then examines how the new technologies challenge old assumptions and support the research on the effectiveness of interactive learning and scholarship. Dr. Van Dusen then takes the reader through an examination of how and why the basic administrative and support systems must be carefully considered if the virtual campus is to be a success. The author's set of seven conclusions and seven recommendations provide a base that institutions can use to implement the new technologies systematically and successfully to support the long-term educational vision of the institution.

Higher education has always been seen as the curator, creator, and critic of the basic knowledge of our world. This basic knowledge is being drastically affected by its rapid transfer through the new electronic channels. The traditional world of higher education must either embrace this new virtual world or become less relevant in the value it adds to society. How effectively institutions link the tools of technology with their educational vision and mission will determine their continued success in being a primary source of education and knowledge for our society. This report on the virtual campus will help institutions engage in conversation concerning their part in the virtual world expanding around us.

Jonathan D. Fife
Series Editor,
Professor of Higher Education Administration, and
Director, ERIC Clearinghouse on Higher Education

ACKNOWLEDGMENTS

For my children:
Kristen, Lauren, Erin, and Steven

INTRODUCTION

The best way to predict the future is to invent it. Alan C.
Kay, Keynote presentation, EDUCOM '88 Conference,
Washington, D.C.

The *virtual campus* is a metaphor for the electronic teaching, learning, and research environment created by the convergence of several relatively new technologies including,
but not restricted to, the Internet, World Wide Web, computer-mediated communication, video conferencing, multimedia, groupware, video-on-demand, desktop publishing,
intelligent tutoring systems, and virtual reality. The melding
of these information and communication technologies has
become possible because of the remarkable growth of computing power, estimated by "Moore's Law" to be doubling
every two years (Barker 1994).

In the literature describing this enriched educational environment, "virtual university," "electronic classroom," and
"virtual classroom" are often used in very specific technological contexts. For example, a virtual or electronic classroom
may refer to a room equipped with multimedia capabilities
or configured for video or computer teleconferencing. In
this monograph, however, "virtual campus" is used more
broadly to epitomize the fundamental cultural and technological transformations that many colleges and universities
are experiencing as a response to a number of internal and
external pressures at the close of the twentieth century.

At the one end of this expansive metaphor is the traditional four-year liberal arts campus, such as Hamilton
College, located on a hilltop in Clinton, New York. Within
this carefully cultivated learning environment, a number of
targeted applications of *instructional technologies,* recently
introduced for the purpose of enhancing existing resources
or addressing "variances from the ideal," in Smallen's (1993,
p. 22) phrase, have taken root among the sheltering oaks of
this "educational Camelot" (p. 22). Technologies such as
electronic discussion groups and computer networking are
incorporated into the curriculum to stimulate traditional
classroom interaction. Additional technologies, such as scientific imaging software, assist students in visualizing complex molecular structures or advanced mathematical models.
Beyond these applications of technology, prep school applicants admitted to the campus can reasonably anticipate the
same kinds of residential living experiences that generations

of alumni have enjoyed since the college's inception in 1812.

At the other end is the true "virtual university," such as Knowledge Network (KN, formerly Mind Extension University), owned by Jones Intercable, the seventh largest cable operator in the United States; or the incipient Western Governors University (WGU; a.k.a. Western Virtual University), perhaps the most ambitious distance learning project in the country. Virtual colleges and universities, like KN or WGU, employ a full range of *distance learning* technologies, such as satellite-delivered telecourses, interactive television, and computer-mediated communications. Delivering courses and even degrees under the auspices of accredited public institutions (like the Universities of Oklahoma, Delaware, and Maryland), KN shares its revenues, presently, as it seeks independent accreditation (Sutton 1996). WGU, on the other hand, draws resources from corporations and higher education institutions in the 15 member states and one territory. Students in these programs, often older working adults, interact with their instructor and with other students, simultaneously or on a delayed basis, from their homes, offices, or other remote sites. In these instances, the traditional classroom has been transmuted into "a crossroads of information flow" (Taitt 1993, p. 3).

Across the spectrum of higher education providers, between the Hamilton Colleges and the Knowledge Networks, are the research institutions, public comprehensive universities, community colleges, and proprietary schools that are poised to reinvent themselves for the information age or, more aptly, for the "Age of Networked Intelligence" (Tapscott 1995b). Most, like St. Louis University and East Carolina University, use instructional technologies to enhance traditional programs (Kalmbach 1994). Others, like California State University, are leveraging technologies to deal with explosive growth in enrollment, projected to surpass one half million by 2005 (West and Daigle 1993). Similar institutions are developing distance learning programs to accommodate the special needs of working adults and other new constituencies (Gross 1995). Distanced interaction serves the needs of traditional students as well, "for skills of collaboration with remote team members will be as central to the future American workplace as performing structured tasks quickly was during the early stages of the industrial revolution" (Dede 1990, p. 247).

Historical Context

It is important to understand the historical context for to-day's virtual campus. Calls for reform based upon the potential of alternative educational media have been heard before (Cuban 1986, 1989; Saettler 1968, 1990).

Support for the integration of visual instructional materials into the curriculum date back at least to 1928 with the publication of Anna Dorris' *Visual Instruction in the Public School* (Saettler 1968). An audiovisual instruction movement flourished in the late 1940s, promoting a modern technological means of providing students with concrete or nonverbal learning experiences (Wagner 1990). The weakness—and ultimate failure—of both reform movements was that they "emphasized materials at the expense of the instruction, and viewed the media as instructional aids rather than as an integral part of the instructional process" (Wagner 1990, p. 11).

The 1950s saw significant economic committment by the federal government and by a private foundation to the development of educational television. The National Defense Education Act (Title VII) of 1958, the Federal Communications Commission, and the Ford Foundation provided vital seed money for research and support of educational programming. When federal funding slowed, instructional use waned (Tyler 1975).

In the 1960s and 1970s the systems models and concepts of educational technology (Banathy 1968; Dick and Carey 1979, 1985) were developed to provide the framework for integrating what we have learned from behavioral science, cognitive psychology, and communication theory. Curriculum and course design have been revolutionized by systems thinking, which promotes the identification of the stages of the instructional design and development process. Systems thinking has produced significant activity in the areas of needs assessment, instructional sequencing, media production and utilization, and goal assessment (Wagner 1990).

Other beneficiaries of the systems approach have been Mastery Learning (Block 1980) and programmed and auto-tutorial instruction (Keller 1968). Such elements as "unit mastery," self-pacing, and the deemphasis of lectures set the stage for later Computer Assisted Instruction (CAI) and, on the virtual campus, Intelligent CAI.

Today, in response to substantial forces at work outside and from within, higher education institutions are poised to invest precious resources on new technologies that may open doors for students and faculty that they did not even know existed.

Pressures on Higher Education Providers

The transfer of these new technologies to the college campus is at the center of a reform movement designed, as the literature suggests, to "transform," "restructure," or "reengineer" higher education administration and instruction (Beaudoin 1990; Bleed 1993; Jensen 1993; Guskin 1994a,b; Heterick 1993; Katz 1993; Massy, Wilger, and Colbeck 1994; Plater 1994; Shapiro 1993; Simpson 1993; Twigg 1993; West and Daigle 1993). The impetus to transform the academy from an industrial to an information paradigm derives from a number of technological, economic, demographic, political, and pedagogical trends:

- *The ubiquity of powerful, affordable personal computers has increased technological resources for teaching, learning, and research.*

With the introduction of the IBM PC in 1981, the hierarchical mainframe culture of the 1960s and 1970s has ceded computing power and institutional data to individuals previously outside the loop (Anadan 1994; Katz 1993). Market forces are producing user-friendly, high-capacity information technologies at ever-declining prices. The computer has become the center or "synthesis device" for a wide assortment of information and telecommunication technologies. The interconnectivity of these devices provides opportunities for advanced instructional and research capabilities (Dede 1990). In 1995, the majority of postsecondary institutions report that most faculty and students "routinely use" personal computers in their academic work (El-Khawas 1995; Green 1996a).

Telecommunications technologies are providing institutions that have distance education programs with new options in response to learners' changing demographic profiles. The new technologies can assist with "problems of scale (not enough students with unusual learning needs in a single location and time), rarity (an instructional specialty not locally available) and cognitive and emotional style (students with visual learning styles can benefit from the multimedia format of distance learning)" (Dede 1990, p. 250).

- *Corporate education programs are assuming a larger share of the higher education function.*

For much of this century, companies have routinely offered programs of apprenticeship or on-the-job training to employees to fill the gap between formal education and the technical competence required for satisfactory job performance. Over the decades, these programs have grown and solidified into a formal system of education and training. In a 1977 report produced for the Conference Board, *Education in Industry,* Lusterman provided a more definitive picture that "left little doubt of the existence of a major educational enterprise in which colleges and universities were (and still are) but little involved" (Lynton 1984, p. 27).

The explosive growth of corporate participation in formal education and training is illustrated by the fact that for 1992, American corporations budgeted 126 million more hours of employee instruction than for the previous year (Davis and Botkin 1994). "This is more growth in just one year than the enrollment growth in all the new conventional college campuses built in the United States between 1960 and 1990" (Tapscott 1995, p. 200).

The implications of corporate education programs for higher education providers are plain. Colleges and universities must adapt the traditional kindergarten-to-college model to the reality of lifelong learning. "The half-life of what a person learns is getting shorter and shorter. Today, half of what an engineer learns as a freshman is effectively obsolete by the time he or she graduates from college and enters the labor force. When you have that speed of change you must upgrade your education throughout your life cycle" (Davis, quoted in "Slicing the Learning Pie" 1996, p. 1).

Furthermore, formal certification procedures will have to keep pace with marketplace requirements. If employers must teach basic skills to recent graduates, the value of traditional certification will be diminished. Colleges and universities must "embrace the new technologies and . . . comprehend what the need is out there that they are serving" (Davis, quoted in "Slicing the Learning Pie" 1996, p. 2). And

"The half-life of what a person learns is getting shorter and shorter. Today, half of what an engineer learns as a freshman is effectively obsolete by the time he or she graduates from college and enters the labor force. . . ."

they must do so on a continuing basis, making certified graduates students for life.

- *Providing resources to match the needs of nontraditional students has created difficulties for an increasing number of higher education institutions.*

The last quarter of the twentieth century has witnessed a steady growth in enrollment at postsecondary institutions and a remarkable increase in the percent of nontraditional students. In 1978, 11.3 million students were enrolled in two- and four-year public and private institutions of higher education; in 1983, 12.5 million; and in 1991, 14.2 million. Enrollment is projected to rise to 16 million by the year 2005 (National Center for Education Statistics [NCES] 1995).

Campus demographic patterns are shifting to reflect a much wider range of student characteristics. Enrollment increases of African American, Hispanic, and Asian American students, particularly at public research and doctoral institutions, have begun to challenge traditional patterns of under-representation (Carter and Wilson 1995). The enrollment of women has increased markedly over the same period, from slightly under 50 percent in 1978 to fully 55 percent by the mid-1990s. The number of older students (25+) has steadily risen to a peak of 44 percent of total enrollment in 1991 (NCES 1995).

The community college "open door" has held particular appeal to nontraditional students. The U.S. Department of Education reported that in 1992-93, of the nearly 5.5 million students enrolled at the more than 1,000 public two-year colleges, 27 percent were students of color (cited by Anandam 1994, p. 4). In addition, community colleges serve substantially more dependent students aged 18-24 with family incomes below $15,000 and, compared to four-year institutions, nearly double the number of students with high school grade point averages of C+ and below (Dougherty 1994, p. 5). Today at most American community colleges, one in three students requires math remediation, and one in four needs English remediation. Nearly 40 percent attend part-time (El-Khawas 1995, p. 23).

On the virtual campus. the problem in providing resources to match the needs of nontraditional students extends to "technology literacy" among students and to their access to computers and networks at home and work. Part-time students, for example, may only be able to access a computer or network from an on-campus lab, and may only get to campus once a week for an evening class.

- *External pressures to provide quantifiable evidence of quality in undergraduate education have left institutions pondering ways to "measure the unmeasurable."*

Prior to 1980, postsecondary institutions defined and measured quality in terms of "inputs"—for example, average SAT scores of successful applicants, the number of faculty possessing doctorates, or the extent of library holdings. With the 1980s came external pressures to assess outcomes, or to document "outputs," including test scores or graduation rates (Chaffee and Sherr 1992). More recently, legislators, employers, and students have demanded that colleges and universities develop stricter measures of accountability and academic productivity.

On the virtual campus, academic productivity is the central rationale for infusing information technology into the educational process. We define productivity here as the ratio of output to the resources invested to produce it. "If a college or university education is the output and if the cost of achieving the same is the measure of input resources, then, adjusted for inflation, higher education has been increasingly less productive for quite some time" (Heterick 1995, p. 1). Will the infusion of technology make institutions more productive? The answer will lie in how these technologies are applied. If they are purchased as bolt-ons to existing processes, improvement in the ratio of output to investment is unlikely. If, however, they are purchased as part of a strategic plan to restructure the institution, improvement in the ratio is possible.

Students, parents, and employers have demanded that the curriculum be more directly relevant to their needs. Students continue to make decisions about attending college not only on the basis of cost but in terms of the benefits received and the time it takes. Furthermore, Altbach (1992) notes that "industries have established formal linkages and research partnerships with universities in order to obtain help with research they feel is important. This relationship has implications for the curriculum as industrial firms have sought to ensure that the skills that they need are incorporated into the curriculum" (p. 49).

Developing valid, reliable measures of quality that satisfy the demands of various external constituencies and that still preserve the traditional autonomy of academic institutions will not be an easy task. To that end a number of institutions are working to establish quantitative approaches that address such elusive, hard-to-define concepts as productivity, efficiency, and effectiveness (Gaither, Nedwek, and Neal 1994). If institutions fail to do so, the prospect exists that externally generated measures will be brought to bear.

Technology and Reform

In its broadest sense, technology is "the knowledge that a civilization has available for adapting and using the environment to fit its needs" (Anandam 1994, p. 3). For the higher education provider, the primary need is "to remain a viable institution in order to serve its students effectively and efficiently and a secondary need is to enhance the productivity of its employees and the quality of the working environment in order to achieve its primary need" (p. 5).

Nationwide, many colleges and universities have sought to remain viable during a period of intense pressure through extremely short-sighted, ad hoc decision making. One such approach is the path of least resistance, downsizing via increasing tuition and fees, cutting nonfaculty positions, cutting part-time faculty, enacting pay cuts, draining active accounts, reducing or freezing library acquisitions, and deferring maintenance (Adams and Palmer 1993). Another approach is to look upon information and communication technologies as the "magic bullet" for reducing costs while simultaneously improving instruction. For example, a review committee at Temple University concluded:

> *Chronically underfunded, ambitious, and stretched thin, Temple nonetheless has planned for and spent money on technology over the last decade for administrative, research and teaching purposes. Although administrative and research computing have benefited from universitywide planning, there has been no planning for the use of technology to improve teaching and learning. Thus, despite the dollars spent, faculty have experienced Temple's policy as what Steve Gilbert has*

*characterized as "lurch, crisis, lurch, crisis." The result
is a system that is out of whack* (Aiken et al 1995, p. 49).

Today the literature of higher education is suffused with
the rhetoric of systemic reform and strategic planning.
Heterick (1993) suggests that for the first time since the in-
vention of moveable type we have "the opportunity and the
technology" to break with the traditional higher education
paradigm, but there are philosophical differences among
theorists and practitioners as to the pace of change:

> *There are those who subscribe to the Mario Andretti
> school of change, "If everything is under control, you
> are going too slow." For them, the occasion of the
> emerging digital technology is reason enough to
> change. A more moderate course of action follows the
> first law of wing walking. "Never let go of what you have
> hold of, until you have hold of something else." Such
> moderates will ask for something more than anecdotal
> evidence that a dramatic shift to digital technology will
> significantly improve either the efficiency or the effec-
> tiveness of teaching and learning. And finally, there are
> those who follow the first law of engineering, "If it ain't
> broke, don't fix it." For the educational conservatives it
> will first be necessary to demonstrate that some, or all,
> of our current approaches are, in fact, broken* (p. 8).

Institutional change carries with it significant political implications. Regardless of leadership philosophy, it cannot be
divorced from the context of students' needs, faculty roles
and responsibilities, society's expectations, legislative constraints, accreditation concerns and, perhaps most importantly, the objectives expressed in one's mission statement.

Thus it is that two distinct reform philosophies emerge
from the literature, each from quite different policy perspectives. The first approach considers educational institutions to
be evolving, with technology performing a support function.
This approach addresses the question, "How can telecommunications be used to assist and extend the ongoing restructuring movement?" (Rockman 1991, p. 28). The second
approach considers educational institutions to be undergoing a revolution, with technology itself responsible for many
of the dramatic changes taking place. This second approach

addresses the question, "How can telecommunications create educational restructuring to increase the productivity and success of schooling?" (Rockman 1991, p. 28). The choice of policy perspectives derives in large part from the ethos of the particular kind of institution.

The ethos of an institution is crystallized in its mission statement, which will vary according to the nature of the institution. While the Carnegie Commission on Higher Education has formulated an elaborate and systematic classification of institutions, for our purposes here there are mainly four kinds: the community college, the liberal arts college, the public comprehensive university, and the research university. Change at an institution is likely to occur when external circumstances influence the institution's capacity to deliver on its mission. For example, a small liberal arts college might emphasize the preparation of generalists for lives of "active citizenship" (Smallen 1993). In this instance, change might merely mean reform which, according to Toombs and Tierney (1991), "denotes a return to a natural or normal state. It connotes a condition in which the direction of change and the final state are known" (p. 9). Thus, a departure in curriculum from the Jeffersonian ideal might prompt an alumni protest, resulting in a reconsideration of the curriculum. On the other hand, change might mean "transformation" which "connotes a metamorphosis" (Toombs and Tierney 1991, p. 9). In the late 1980s, for example, an announcement by the National Science Foundation of plans to create a new national high-speed data communications network resulted in new emphasis by research universities on network connectivity that would "increase campus computing integration and mitigate the complexities of a fragmented and diverse computing environment" (Katz 1993, p. 17). In both cases, change occurred in response to external pressures to "reform" or "transform," consistent with the stated objectives of the institution. In general, reform literature makes no such linguistic distinctions, though in most instances such distinctions are crucial to the success of the innovation.

Calls for significant educational reform based upon the potential of technology must address the integrative nature of change within an organization. When an innovation is successfully integrated, it becomes institutionalized; that is, it is supported by and integrated into other aspects of the organization (Curry 1992). Institutionalization is a gradual process, not the result of administrative fiat. Cuban (1986) observes that past failed attempts to integrate technological solutions to educational problems tend to follow a cycle. First, there is a period of excitement and unreasonable claims—what Rockman calls "technohype" (1991, p. 25). This period is followed by one of very low-level implementation, with relatively marginal participation by faculty and staff. Last, frustration and disillusionment lead to relegating the technology to "add-on" status or a dusty death on a closet shelf (see also Green and Gilbert 1995).

Today, there is again a pressing call for technology to provide expanded higher educational opportunities to a very wide spectrum of present and potential clientele. The task of integrating the new technologies into the mainstream of post-secondary teaching and learning, not to mention the broader organizational culture, is all the more daunting because of numerous obstacles and competing interests, which include:

1. A lack of adequate leadership at all levels of implementation (Kearsley and Lynch 1992).
2. Overt resistance from an entrenched faculty and administrative culture, 700 years in the making (Altbach 1992).
3. Deemphasis of teaching over research, especially in tenure and promotion decisions (Cartwright 1994b; Keig and Waggoner 1994).
4. An increasing number of part-time faculty (El-Khawas 1995) without adequate technical training or support (Digranes and Digranes 1995).
5. Inadequate startup and ongoing funding (Krebs 1996).

These and other obstacles illustrate Darby's (1992) contention that "the primary constraint is neither technical nor pedagogical but organizational and social in nature" (p. 195).

Overcoming such obstacles requires technology leadership that permeates the organization from top to bottom. People involved in the change process—administrators, faculty, students, and staff—must at least informally accept responsibility for encouraging and supporting each other in the use of technology to solve pressing problems. They must believe in what they are doing, be willing to support the allocation of resources for technological solutions, and have access to prerequisite technical expertise (Kearsley and Lynch 1992).

The Organization of the Report

The focus of this monograph is of necessity limited to changes occurring in higher education institutions that are committed to reform via technology. A survey of the literature finds reform characterized by changes in teaching, learning, research and scholarly activity, organizational culture, and governance and finance. Section two takes up teaching on the virtual campus and how institutional variables influence adoption of information technologies according to their particular missions and goals. Section three, on classroom learning, contrasts traditional and virtual classrooms and describes the interface capabilities of various technologies. Section four explores recent reconceptualizations of scholarship as well as new computer-based technologies that are beginning to influence both the methods and substance of research. Section five depicts efforts to reform both the bureaucratic and academic spheres of higher education institutions by applying principles of Total Quality Management. Section six delineates some of the important new responsibilities of governing boards, including monitoring regulatory legislation, establishing a telecommunications policy, and shepherding resources for technology. The final section draws conclusions from the literature and makes recommendations for institutional planning and research.

TEACHING ON THE VIRTUAL CAMPUS:
NEW ROLES, NEW RESPONSIBILITIES

> *This instrument can teach. It can illuminate, yes, and it can even inspire. But it can do so only to the extent that humans are determined to use it to those ends. Otherwise, it's nothing but wires and lights in a box.* Edward R. Murrow, referring to the early potential of radio (quoted by Gross, Muscarella, and Pirkl 1994, p. 139).

The European university model, first established in 13th-century France, has remained for 700 years the "one common academic model worldwide" (Altbach 1992, p. 40). The resilience of this model, as evidenced by recurring adaptation to changing circumstances, is all the more remarkable when we consider that of 70 institutions dating back to the Reformation, 67 are colleges and universities (Ernst, Katz, and Sack 1994).

At the center of this Paris model is *le professeur,* whose academic autonomy became solidified in the institutional ethos seven centuries ago (Altbach 1992). Deriving power not from the ability to teach or conduct research but from the right to certify and examine, the professor determined the period of study for students in residence (Toombs and Tierney 1991). In medieval Scotland and later in colonial America, curriculum took shape and a credit-for-contact model was established; student progress became a function of hours clocked in the lecture hall, seminar room, or laboratory. The model, or paradigm, acquired a number of very specific attributes, which continue today. In the Instruction Paradigm (Barr and Tagg 1995; Boggs 1995-96; Gilbert 1995; O'Banion 1995-96), the professor imparts selected knowledge, primarily through live lecture and discussion, and sorts students into categories based upon achievement or merit. Students sit passively during lecture, participate sporadically in discussions, toil individually with assignments, and struggle competitively during examinations. Instructional technologies, if and when applied, play a support function. Classes, meeting typically for 50 minutes a session, begin around Labor Day and end before Memorial Day each year.

Reflecting on the shortcomings of such a system, Carl Rogers anticipated the pivotal issue almost 50 years ago:

> *If instead of focusing all our interest on the teacher—What shall I teach? How can I prove that I have taught it? How can I "cover" all that I should teach?—we fo-*

---

cused our interest on the student, the questions and the issues would all be different. Suppose we asked, what are his purposes in this course, what does he wish to learn, how can we facilitate his learning and growth? A very different type of education would ensue (cited in Bonwell and Eison 1991, p. 63).

"Ironically," as Gross (1995) observes about the Instruction Paradigm, "we have known for years that this is not the best way to teach" (p. 30). Numerous obstacles and competing interests, outlined earlier, have prevented faculty and institutions from exploring a broader array of instructional options. As an industrial model of efficiency, the large lecture hall was deemed appropriate for a labor-intensive environment.

Instruction Versus Learning Paradigms
Today's virtual campus serves various constituencies in different ways. The Instruction Paradigm continues to define policy and practice for many higher education providers, particularly four-year liberal arts institutions. Increasingly, however, new information and communication technologies meliorate the residential collegiate experience by improving educational services. Students register, access transcripts, apply for financial aid, locate resources, and communicate after class with professors and fellow students through technological links. Live lectures, presentations, and discussions remain the dominant mode of classroom instruction, but new technologies play an increasingly prominent role.

Other institutions have begun to transform educational policy and practice by emphasizing student learning outcomes and by restructuring the work of faculty members (Barr and Tagg 1995; Gilbert 1995; Guskin 1994). In the Learning Paradigm, educational providers have shifted the focus from providing instruction to producing learning (Barr and Tagg 1995; Boggs 1995; O'Banion 1995-96). The role of the professor has shifted from lecturer to coach and mentor (Gross 1995). A paradigm shift is now possible because faculty have available powerful new tools to wed theory to practice. A substantial research base has evolved to extend our knowledge of learning: instructional design processes; cognitive, affective, and physiological learning styles; distance learning theory; adult learning theory (androgogy); and active and cooperative learning strategies. Interactive learning resources such as on-line computers and comprehensive multimedia have created many new venues for teaching and learning. As the Learning Paradigm matures, the role of the professor will change and possibly even be radically transformed. According to one such scenario, "the professor" is replaced by "the specialist" who "will be employed on a contract basis to produce specific products or deliver specific services; many will work part-time, often from their homes, linked to learners through technology" (O'Banion 1995-96, p. 23). National faculty unions such as the National Education Association (NEA), the American Federation of Teachers (AFT), and the American Association of University Professors (AAUP) have already begun to address issues concerning technology and organizational changes in their publications (Gilbert 1995) and to exhort locals to remain vigilant regarding attempts to unilaterally impose changes involving working conditions (Task Force on Technology in Higher Education 1996).

Clearly, before a true paradigmatic shift is likely to occur, technology leaders within and outside the academy will have to grapple with a number of crucial issues, a few of which are succinctly articulated by Merchant (1995):

> *What knowledge is worth knowing in the context of an increasingly diverse society nested within a global economy? Who decides what knowledge is to be measured and how will it be measured? What should schools look like, with respect to their organization for teaching and learning? Who should participate in decisions affecting the educational experiences of students and what should this participation look like? What are the consequences of specific educational policies and practices for the different participants?* (p. 268).

"Ironically," as Gross (1995) observes about the Instruction Paradigm, "we have known for years that this is not the best way to teach" (p. 30). As an industrial model of efficiency, the large lecture hall was deemed appropriate for a labor-intensive environment.

Institutional Variables

Smallen (1993) describes an ideal learning environment as one having two fundamental characteristics: "subject engagement—consistent opportunities for students to actively engage subject matter—and interaction—consistent opportunities for students to interact with other students and the instructor to test their own ideas and to learn from the ideas of others" (p. 23). Furthermore, Smallen advances a thesis that serves as a crucible to test the effectiveness of information technology applications within the context of different institutional missions:

> *Successful applications of technology to the learning process, at any institution, will be ones that address variances from the ideal learning environment. Technology applied in a manner oblivious to these variances will not improve teaching and learning, and will waste critical institutional resources* (p. 22).

Against this standard, we can begin to measure effectiveness in terms of how the new technologies assist institutions in fulfilling their unique missions.

Postsecondary institutions vary in adopting information technologies for classroom use according to their particular missions and goals. In the United States, four types of higher education institutions predominate: the four-year liberal arts college, the American research university, the public comprehensive university, and the community college.

The four-year liberal arts college

For many Americans, the small liberal arts college represents the ideal environment in which to develop intellectually. Small classes, individual attention, and accessibility of faculty and staff create a milieu that has been likened to an "educational Camelot" (Pew Research Report, cited by Smallen 1993, p. 22). The philosophy of a liberal arts college is to prepare students for "active citizenship":

> *This preparation is accomplished through the development of fundamental analytical and communication skills, rather than through training for a particular occupation. A liberal arts education is based upon the premise that the future is, at best, uncertain, and that generalists rather than those with specific training are best prepared to deal with that uncertainty. Further, the liberal arts education is concerned with preparation for a "lifetime" of learning* (Smallen 1993, p. 23).

On the liberal arts campus, targeted applications of technology are used to expand student learning opportunities. For example, electronic mail can enhance communication between faculty and student when other time and place constraints exist. And in those instances where interaction languishes in the occasional larger class, information technologies such as guided discussion software and campus computer networks can stimulate student interaction. Furthermore, demonstrably effective laboratory simulations that multiply opportunities for subject matter engagement would be another area where new technologies can make inroads (Land and LoPerfido 1993).

The American research university

If the liberal arts college can be likened to "an educational Camelot," the modern American research university may be regarded as "a sheltered grove in which knowledge is propagated, created, and applied" (Atkinson and Tuzin, quoted by Katz 1993, p. 13). The uniqueness of higher education research institutions is epitomized by five "defining characteristics": (1) corporatization, with external boards safeguarding public subsidies, (2) faculty orientation toward applied research and practical classroom instruction, (3) issuance of doctoral degrees, (4) federally sponsored scientific research, and (5) provision of higher education opportunities to traditionally disenfranchised segments of the population, particularly after the Second World War. Although other higher education institutions may possess one or more of these characteristics, only the American research university combines all five (Katz 1993).

Driving the current explosion of technology is campus-wide emphasis on research, which, according to one estimate, supplies "almost half of the nation's basic research [and] about 28 percent of its total research" (*In the National Interest,* quoted in Katz 1993, p. 14). Although federal support continues to be a factor, now a growing segment of users of technology and a huge portion of the demand come from undergraduate and faculty outside the sphere of federal support. The new technologies have made the transition from the unique to the ubiquitous.

This emphasis on research has influenced pedagogical theory in two profound ways. First, faculty participation in research activities is thought to impact the quality of instruction:

> *This premise suggests a "trickle down" model of knowledge propagation in which (1) faculty enthusiasm*

about the process of discovery is exported to the class-
room, (2) student learning is enhanced directly by
access to research activities and by-products, and (3)
curricula devised by active researchers better reflect a
discipline's state of the art (Katz 1993, p. 15).

Second, graduate students engaged in original research
come to value access to up-to-date technology, according to
one survey, even more than interaction with faculty mentors
(Katz 1993). Thus, the proposition that interaction is a fundamental component of higher education instruction may be
significantly less true for graduate students at research institutions than for their undergraduate counterparts at other
types of institutions.

The American research university invested early and
heavily in information technology since the first wave of
campus computing, 1947-1977 (Hawkins 1991, p. 160).
While mainframe access, on a time-sharing basis, gradually
grew, it was not until academic departments and laboratories became the locus of personal computing in the 1980s
that various new ancillary technologies began to have widespread impact on all sectors of teaching, learning, and research (Katz 1993).

The public comprehensive university

Like research institutions, public comprehensive universities
were a response to fundamental societal change. On the one
hand, research universities embraced applied knowledge
and experimentation in response to the growing commer-
cialism and expansionism following the Civil War (Katz
1993). By contrast, the public comprehensive university
came into existence as a response to the democratization of
higher education following the Second World War (West and
Daigle 1993). Spurred by substantial state and federal investment, including direct financial aid to students, these bur-
geoning institutions attempted to become all things to all
people. West and Daigle (1993) have suggested that they
have indeed become the "mall[s] of higher education where
learners stop in and out and have choices from a wide range
of academic programs designed to prepare them for the
professional and technical workplace or for graduate education" (p. 24).

Many public comprehensive universities are contemplating leveraging information technologies to address increased enrollment demands. For example, at the nation's largest system, California State University, enrollment tops 360,000 on 20 campuses spread over nearly 1,000 miles. As system enrollment is projected to increase approximately 150,000 over the next decade, tens of thousands of students will "attend" virtual classrooms. An increasingly older, ethnically and racially diverse constituency will further strain the system's traditional resources (West and Daigle 1993).

The challenge to maintain quality during times of upheaval will be met by institutions with vision and with commitments from campus constituencies to do more with seemingly less. At California State University, the search for alternative strategies led to the formation of Project Delta (Direct Electronic Learning Teaching Alternative), which "may challenge many traditional assumptions, policies, and practices concerning the nature of higher education in the next century" (West and Daigle 1993, p. 38). As public comprehensive universities—like California State University—attempt to reengineer themselves for the Information Age, faculty will play a crucial role in addressing what may prove to be enormous "variances from the ideal learning environment" (Smallen 1993, p. 22).

The community college

The largest and easily the most volatile segment of higher education is the community college, conceived in 1901 as a "junior" college. Enrolling an estimated 5.5 million students by 1995 and capturing nearly 40 percent of the higher education market (NCES 1995), community colleges can be expected to be a major player in employing new technologies to "harness the winds of change" (Bleed 1993, p. 28).

The community college is a particularly fertile setting in which to explore and develop the capabilities of information technologies for educational purposes. With its "open door" admissions policy, small classes, and focus on teaching and learning—rather than on research—the community college is poised to balance the interests of the individual with the needs of the larger community. Community colleges have long been the leaders among higher education institutions in providing innovative programs to diverse clients. As Bleed succinctly puts it, "While elitist institutions have defined their excellence in terms that are exclusionary, community colleges have sought to define their excellence in the service to many" (1993, p. 28). This mandate has special implications for the use of information and instructional technologies; the new learning infrastructure can offer instruction in a flexible, modular form. "Learners' schedules and learning styles may not match institutional schedules and instructors' pedagogical styles, and time may be wasted covering topics already mastered in previous course work" (Graves 1994, p. 4).

Historically, community colleges have responded to diversity in a number of ways. To meet the needs of high school dropouts and the academically deficient, community colleges have made substantial commitments to both labor-intensive developmental programs and computer-assisted instruction. For students constrained by time, distance, or childcare, colleges have experimented with various distance learning venues, such as prepackaged telecourses and correspondence courses. Over the past decade, however, the open door has expanded to welcome students who are "more heavily working class, minority, female, and older than are four-year college students" (Dougherty 1994, p. 3). The needs of these students, as well as the growing number of middle-income, middle- and upper-ability students opting for two years at community colleges as a way to save money, will place additional strains on institutions already forced by budget cuts to do more with less.

As community colleges attempt to deal with greater diversity, they will also be forced to respond in a proactive way to major trends reshaping the nation's economy. Four trends in particular require community colleges to rethink their positions on how to deliver "relevant training to currently employed workers whose skills need upgrading" as well as to students who are currently unemployed: "(1) the downsizing occurring in many companies, (2) the growing move to the outsourcing of work and services, (3) the increasing use of a 'contingent' workforce, and (4) an increasing disparity between people who have completed college and those who have only a high school degree" (Pennington 1994, p. 1).

Standing at "the intersection of education, jobs, economic development, workforce preparation, and reform" (Pennington 1994, p. 4) the community college instructor must function as facilitator for students preparing for workforce realities. Among the continuing challenges to instructors will be: (1) to leverage the information and telecommunications technologies for providing students the technical and career-related competencies, (2) to join in partnerships with K-12 feeder school teachers and university faculty, and (3) to play an expanded institutional role in forging alliances with business and industry personnel.

An Agenda for Professional Development

Institutional variables have been and are likely to remain the critical element in defining faculty roles and responsibilities. Teaching cannot be isolated from context. Historically, successful instructors have been able to draw upon their own resources, regardless of institutional climate, to build a repertoire of effective teaching techniques. However, in an era of networked intelligence, a student-centered learning environment will demand of faculty a knowledge of innovative applications of technology as well as a wide range of facilitative roles.

Traditional faculty development—in the form of professional programs and conferences, in-service workshops, and department meetings—will remain an important vehicle for evaluating and implementing existing and new technologies. On the virtual campus, however, the new technologies themselves—for example, the Internet and World Wide Web—will assume a greater role in the delivery of professional development, thus serving as a model of the very elements of a student-centered learning environment discussed earlier. Among the many types of resources designed to enhance professional development and found on the Internet are (1) professional association homepages; (2) peer comparison information; and (3) listservs, newsgroups, and e-mail discussion groups.

Hundreds of professional associations and discipline-specific organizations have a Web presence. Each offers a Web site or gopher site with professional development resources, including information about membership, upcoming conferences, and publications. An especially useful feature of this homepage is the electronic conference program, which provides detailed information on paprs, panels, and topics of interest. Other kinds of useful information include e-mail addresses for organizational members and elected officers and a calendar of future events.

The Web also offers an array of data and information for peer institution comparisons. If professional development activities involve student learning and assessment, homepages of peer institutions may yield fruitful links to similar activities on other campuses. Such homepages are dynamic and evolving, so it's wise to visit the sites regularly for changes and updates.

Another Internet resource with unlimited potential for professional development is the listserv, newsgroup, or e-mail discussion group. Although the delivery mechanisms vary, in essence each serves as an asynchronous forum for electronic discussion or data exchange.

Regardless of the delivery method used for professional development—in-service workshop or electronic forum—professional development coordinators need to be mindful of a number of critical variables that influence faculty adoption of an innovation:

1. Relative advantage—the degree to which an innovation is perceived as better than the idea it supersedes;
2. Compatibility—the degree to which an innovation is perceived as being consistent with existing values, past experiences, and needs of potential adopters;
3. Complexity—the degree to which an innovation is perceived as difficult to understand and use;
4. Trialability—the degree to which an innovation could be experimented with on a limited basis; and
5. Observability—the degree to which the results of an innovation are visible to others (Rogers, quoted in Bonwell and Eison 1991, p. 71).

Mindful of these variables, the professional development coordinator can begin to fashion an agenda reflective of the ethos of the particular institution. Such a preliminary agenda should at least include (1) learning styles of students, (2) distance learning theory, (3) instructional design processes, (4) adult learning theory, and (5) active and cooperative learning.

Learning styles of students
A learning style refers to the way a student absorbs, processes, and retains information (Claxton and Murrell 1987). When learning styles are at odds with traditional classroom teaching strategies, learning may be compromised (Dunn, Beaudry, and Klavas 1989). The value of including learning styles on the professional development agenda is threefold: (1) in a student-centered system, information

about learning styles provides faculty with a broader profile of the learner than can be deduced by test scores or grade point average (Keefe 1987), (2) understanding the ways students learn can help the instructor/facilitator become more responsive to the differences students bring to the classroom, and (3) knowledge about learning styles is a critical early component in the instructional design process (Dick and Carey 1985; Gagne 1985).

Learning styles can be classified as cognitive, affective, and physiological behaviors (Keefe 1987). Cognitive styles are information-processing habits or behaviors that students use to think, solve problems, and remember (Messick 1984). More than a dozen dimensions of cognitive style exist in the literature of experimental research, including field independence/dependence, tolerance for incongruity, categorizing, complexity vs. simplicity, and automatization (Keefe 1987). Affective learning styles consist of the learner's emotional predispositions, including measures of self-confidence, tolerance, curiosity, anxiety risk-taking, and need for structure and guidelines (Keefe 1987). Finally, physiological styles involve visual, auditory, tactile, and kinesthetic behavior preferences in particular learning environments and may include specific preferences for lighting conditions, seating comfort, tactile manipulation of materials under study, and so forth (Keefe 1987).

Becoming more responsive to student needs may result in designing learning experiences that match or deliberately mismatch student learning styles:

> *Matching is particularly appropriate in working with poorly prepared students and with new college students, as the most attrition occurs in these situations. Some studies show that identifying a student's style and then providing instruction consistent with that style contribute to more effective learning.*
>
> *In other instances, some mismatching may be appropriate so that students' experiences help them to learn in new ways and to bring into play ways of thinking and aspects of the self not previously developed* (Claxton and Murrell 1987, p. iii).

In a student-centered system, faculty need to reach beyond traditional methods and begin to explore strategies that respond to the individual needs of students.

In a student-centered system, faculty need to reach beyond traditional methods and begin to explore strategies that respond to the individual needs of students.

Distance learning theory

On many college campuses, an experimental laboratory for the application of technology to dynamic new learning environments already exists in the innovative programs provided by distance education. For many years, distance education has brought educational services to typically older, nontraditional students through state-of-the-art media, including microwave, satellite, cablecast, and telephone lines. The growth of new technologies, such as computer-mediated communication, interactive television, the Internet and the World Wide Web, has revolutionized distance learning.

Distance education faculty have much to contribute to a program of professional development. In most instances, faculty are recruited from traditional disciplines to teach courses at a distance (Levine 1992). As content specialists and technology users, distance education instructors are uniquely positioned to provide leadership on technology-related issues. Kearsley and Lynch (1992) note that "much instructional technology leadership comes from teachers who have informally accepted responsibility for encouraging and supporting teachers, students, and staff in their use of technology. . . . The main advantage is that such leadership is driven by genuine conviction and first-hand experience" (p. 54). College faculty are more likely to respond to peers, especially within the same or similar discipline, who have something new to say about teaching and learning (Keig and Waggoner 1994).

Keig and Waggoner (1994) cite Mathis who notes that professional development consultants are frequently psychologists whose expertise is outside the specific disciplines of those they purport to "counsel," thus producing cultural resistance:

> *Those who organize institutional programs for instructional development should be aware of the 'culture' of the many disciplines in higher education. While psychology may have much to say about teaching and learning, psychologists are not always able to communicate this to their colleagues outside of psychology in a language easily accepted or understood. The value of having faculty in the many fields of study who know the research literature on teaching and learning, and who can communicate with their colleagues in the*

language of their discipline, suggests that instructional development can best be served by preparing faculty to perform an instructional development function in their own field rather than anticipating salvation from a central hive populated with psychologists (Mathis, quoted in Keig and Waggoner 1994. p. 38).

By utilizing in-house resources—namely distance education programs and faculty—institutions can increase faculty receptivity to the kinds of interactive learning opportunities afforded by telecommunications technology. Improved teaching—a primary goal of professional development—will occur "when faculty support each other with expertise that is uniquely theirs, apart from what students, teaching consultants, and academic administrators can contribute to instructional improvement" (Keig and Waggoner 1994, p. 15).

Instructional design processes

Teaching on the virtual campus will require of traditional instructors an initial investment of time on instructional design considerations, including the coordination of crucially important variables. Instructional design is based on a systematic approach where all parts affect all other parts (in fact, instructional development was often referred to as the "systems" approach). It is an iterative process where each time an instructor redesigns a course it gets better based on many factors. It is unlikely to be "perfect" the first time out. In short, the instructional design process provides a way of thinking about a course.

As a domain of instructional technology, instructional design is "the process of specifying the conditions for learning" (Seels and Richey 1995, p. 30). The process is intended to identify "exactly what needs to be learned, the most efficient and effective manner in which it can be taught, and to design an instructional system that matches these requirements" (Eastmond and Ziegahn 1995, p. 61). Many such design systems or models, based upon findings in behavioral psychology, are in use today (Dick and Carey 1985; Haynes and Dillon 1992; Heinich, Molenda, and Russell 1989; Romiszowski 1981; Wagner 1990). For alternative learning environments, such as interactive television or on-line, computer-mediated classrooms, any conventional design model can serve as a useful benchmark.

New models of instructional design, targeting adult learners working in alternative learning environments, have recently been developed (Eastmond and Zieghan 1995; Price and Repman 1995). These new "facilitation" models of course design, underpinned by adult learning theory, "encourage adults to be more self-directing throughout the instructional process; capitalize on their experiences, strengths and interests; and enable them to apply whatever knowledge and skills they learn to their own problem solving or developmental task" (Eastmond and Ziegahn 1995, p. 61). Price and Repman (1995) propose a nine-step design model, which includes (1) identifying course goals, (2) analyzing and organizing content, (3) writing performance objectives, (4) identifying learner characteristics, (5) developing lesson plans, (6) developing and selecting instructional materials, (7) designing and conducting formative evaluation, (8) conducting instruction and modifying instructional plans, and (9) designing and conducting summative evaluation. Eastmond and Ziegahn's (1995) model follows five stages: (1) technical production, training and support; (2) instructional course development; (3) instructor training; (4) course delivery; and (5) evaluation and revision.

In order to address variances from the ideal learning environment, such as instances where students are at a physical distance from the instructor or where technology must leverage large numbers of students simultaneously,Moore and Thompson (1990) contend that four variables in particular—humanizing, participation, message style, and feedback—need to be incorporated into the instructional design process:

Humanizing refers to the creation of an accepting environment which breaks down the barrier of distance and generates feelings of rapport between teacher and students. Participation deals with the extent of interaction among participants in the interactive situation. Message style refers to ways of enhancing the interest and appeal of a presentation. Planning for short instructional segments, varying tone of voice and volume, and supplementing programs with visual aids maintain the interest and attention of the students. Feedback allows instructors to determine if their presentations were clear and effective. Both verbal and written feed-

*back should be obtained, and can include question-
naires, interviews, or group reports* (quoted by Price
and Repman 1995, p. 255).

Instructional design is an important topic for professional
development activities. Fruitful learning experiences should
not be accidental. Programs, workshops, and professional
conferences can assist the traditional instructor to manage
the design and coordinate the variables that make one class
a more rewarding and successful experience than another.

Adult learning theory
In recent years, demographic and economic realities have
challenged postsecondary institutions, particularly community
colleges and university branch campuses, to focus upon
workplace education and access to skills and knowledge for
underrepresented constituencies. At community colleges nationwide, older, nontraditional students (women who are
reentering the work force, ethnic minorities, and workers who
are disabled or displaced) outnumber those from all other
higher education institutions combined (Dougherty 1994).
Meeting the needs of adult learners will require of college
instructors at least a rudimentary awareness of adult education literature as well as of the growing body of research on
adult learning theory and practice. Professional development
activities can provide a valuable orientation to the new roles
and responsibilities required of adult educators.
The literature of adult education is replete with reference
to androgogy, "the art and science of helping adults learn"
(Knowles 1984, p. 43), which is usually contrasted with pedagogy, the art and science of helping children learn.
According to Knowles (1984), adult learners possess six
characteristics distinct from younger learners:

1. *The learner's self-concept.* Adults have a self-concept of
   being responsible for their own decisions, for their own
   lives. Once they have arrived at that self-concept, they
   develop a deep psychological need to be seen by others
   and treated by others as being capable of self-direction.
2. *The role of the learner's experience.* Adults come into an
   education activity with both a greater volume and a
   different quality of experience than younger learners.
3. *Readiness to learn.* Adults are ready to learn those

things they need to know and be able to do in order to cope effectively with their real-life situations.

4. *Orientation to learning.* Adults are problem-centered, or life-centered, in their orientation to learning. Adults are motivated to devote energy to learning to the extent they perceive the learning will help them perform tasks or deal with problems that they confront in their life situations.

5. *Need to know.* Adults need to know why they should learn something before beginning to learn it.

6. *Motivation.* While adults are responsive to some external motivators, the best motivators are internal, such as self-esteem, quality of life, and desire for increased job satisfaction (Cennamo and Dawley 1995, p. 15).

Knowles (1984) contends that adult educators, teaching in various settings, need to function more as facilitators than content experts. Hayes (1990) summarizes the responsibilities of this new role: "As facilitators, they should involve adult learners in a collaborative process of diagnosing learning needs, planning and conducting educational activities, and evaluating outcomes. Organization of content should be problem centered rather than subject centered, and experiential learning activities should be stressed" (p. 32).

As the number and needs of nontraditional students increase in various institutional settings, college instructors can be expected to access an array of instructional strategies to prepare students for a changing job market. A knowledge of and sensitivity to what the learner brings to the doorstep of higher education can be used to serve that end.

Active and cooperative learning

In an authentic student-centered system of instruction, the student's role is redefined as well as the instructor's. Each student can be expected to do far more than sit back in class "listening to teachers, memorizing prepackaged assignments, and spitting out answers"; they "must talk about what they are learning, write about it, relate it to past experiences, apply it to their daily lives. They must make what they learn part of themselves" (Chickering and Gamson 1987, p. 3). Active learning and cooperative learning, two established classroom techniques designed for virtually any kind of classroom environment, are especially well suited to the demands of the virtual classroom.

Active learning, though never very precisely defined in the literature, has been aptly described as "anything that involves students in doing things and thinking about the things they are doing" (Bonwell and Eison 1991, p. 2). Active learning techniques often produce a scenario very different from the ones associated with the traditional classroom:

> *Students are involved in more than listening.*
> *Less emphasis is placed on transmitting information and more on developing students' skills.*
> *Students are involved in higher-order thinking (analysis, synthesis, evaluation).*
> *Students are engaged in activities (e.g. reading, discussing, writing).*
> *Greater emphasis is placed on students' exploration of their own attitudes and values* (Bonwell and Eison 1991, p. 2).

The variety of today's educational technologies make possible many of the classroom techniques recommended by proponents of active learning: impromptu writing, student-generated questioning, small group discussion, demonstrations, simulations, role playing, games, debates, drama, and peer teaching (Bonwell and Eison 1991).

Cooperative learning, an active learning strategy, refers to "the instructional use of small groups so that students work together to maximize their own and each other's learning" (Johnson, Johnson and Smith 1991, p. iii). Cooperative learning involves more than grouping students for purposes of discussion and collaborative projects. Three kinds of learning groups—formal, informal, and base—can be organized for teaching specific content, for providing a mechanism for analysis and feedback, and for continuous support and academic assistance (p. 9). Designed originally for traditional classroom settings, cooperative learning techniques can be adapted to an electronic environment via the interactive capabilities of two-way video and computer-mediated communications. Telecommunications technology makes possible synchronous (real time) video or on-line discussion groups as well as asynchronous (delayed) exchanges via electronic bulletin boards and mail.

Active learning and cooperative learning can provide instructors with a conceptual framework for developing various kinds of student-centered classroom activities. Professional development workshops can serve as the catalyst for facilitating the transition from a traditional lecture-oriented classroom to an electronic, highly interactive learning environment.

Summary

A paradigmatic shift in education, based upon a technological breakthrough, is not without precedent. The most often cited example is the printing press, which became an enabling technology for millions of newly literate Europeans. The impact of mass-produced books "changed both the educational system and the class structure, with consequences that still shape our attitudes today" (Berge and Collins 1995, p. 2). Presently, we are witness to a dramatic transformation in American business and industry, fueled in large part by the explosion of information made available by digital technologies. Repercussions have already been and are continuing to be felt on college campuses, traditionally slow to react to external influence. The most significant result, the literature suggests, with long-range consequences for colleges, universities, and society at large, is the paradigmatic shift from a professor-centered to a student-centered system of learning. The implications for the profession of teaching are far-reaching.

One implication of the paradigmatic shift for the profession of teaching is a recommitment to creating an ideal learning environment for students, employing new technologies to address variances from that environment. The degree of variance will depend upon other variables, including the type of institution providing the instruction. Liberal arts colleges, public comprehensive and research universities, and community colleges can all be expected to fully exploit the new technologies in accordance with their institutional missions.

A second major implication for the profession of teaching is a shift from traditional to new roles and classroom responsibilities. The transition from lecturer to facilitator will not happen overnight and will be accompanied by institutional and professional commitments to incorporate research findings into professional development activities. Beyond merely providing technical training in the latest (and soon obsolete technology, professional development activities will need to focus on crucial classroom variables that will ultimately determine the level of productive interaction and intellectual engagement apropos to the individual and group.

One implication of the paradigmatic shift for the profession of teaching is a recommitment to creating an ideal learning environment for students, employing new technologies to address variances from that environment.

CLASSROOM LEARNING: INTERACTION AND INTERFACE

I hear and I forget; I see and I remember; I do and I understand.
    –Chinese proverb

As far back as the Middle Ages, constraints of time and distance have been decisive factors for students of higher education. Until the end of the 12th century, students wandered from country to city, from monastery to cathedral to hear a celebrated lecturer or to study a particular subject under the tutelage of a master who determined the time and the place of instruction (Murray 1978; Tannenbaum 1971). Thus, even before universities were formally organized into centers of learning, the die had been cast: students would learn in the manner and under the conditions prescribed by the professor, and eventually by the institution.

Today the Instruction Paradigm continues to serve the traditional age cohort, the 18 to 25 year old, much as it has for generations of college students. However, a number of recent trends outlined in section one of this monograph have put pressure on institutions to provide educational services in the manner and under conditions prescribed by the institution's new client, the "new century" student. By empowering students to determine the venue—"anyway, anywhere, anytime" (O'Banion 1995-96, p. 22)—a new Learning Paradigm is now possible. In this section, three key issues are considered: (1) What are the structural components of the traditional classroom experience and what unrealized potential remains for this learning environment? (2) How are these same structural components affected by the introduction of information and communication technologies? and (3) How are technologies selected to fulfill the needs of newly empowered students?

The Traditional Classroom
The four structural components of the classroom experience are time, space, people and knowledge (Blount 1995, p. 198). Historically, one of the severest criticisms of higher education has been that "conventional delivery systems create an educational caste structure in which the economically, geographically, or socially privileged have sole access" (Reed and Sork 1990, p. 4). In the traditional higher education paradigm, time (of class) and distance (from campus) have prevented many individuals from attending college, full- or part-

time. Hezel and Dirr (1991) found that older, nontraditional students surveyed were prevented from attending traditional classes on campus due to work and family responsibilities and, to a lesser degree, transportation and childcare problems. Though nearly all the respondents in another study preferred mixed-age classrooms and the diverse points of view shared (Lynch and Bishop-Clark 1994), the traditional age cohort (18-25) continues to make up the majority of college students in traditional classroom settings (NCES 1995).

For students able to overcome barriers of time and space, the traditional classroom provides the locus for much of what they will learn. The remaining structural elements of the classroom, people and knowledge, permit a triad of potential interaction: learner-content, learner-instructor, and learner-learner (Moore 1989a). Learner-content interaction is the hallmark of education; "without it there cannot be education, since it is the process of intellectually interacting with content that results in change in the learner's understanding, the learner's perspective, or the cognitive structures of the learner's mind" (Moore 1989a, p. 2). Students begin an "internal dialogue" with this material, producing a new awareness and new level of understanding. Content itself is typically supplied through textbooks and lecture notes, but it may come in other forms, depending upon the resourcefulness of the instructor and the student.

In the traditional college classroom, the dominant mode of learner-instructor interaction is lecture, or lecture and discussion, particularly for introductory courses such as biology, psychology, and math (Ellsworth 1995). Philosophic support for the lecture format is customarily attributed to John Locke's epistemology as set forth in his 1690, *An Essay Concerning Human Understanding:* "Let us suppose the mind to be, as we say, white paper, void of all characters, without any idea." The proposition that the human mind is a blank sheet of paper, a *tabula rasa,* onto which information can be transcribed, is an easy metaphor to seize, especially for the lecturer inexperienced with other methodologies. Lectures do, in fact, have the advantage of distilling a great deal of disparate information that would be inaccessible or otherwise unreasonably time-consuming to locate. Furthermore, when skillfully presented, a good lecture can motivate an audience to pursue the subject further, independently (Johnson, Johnson, and Smith 1991).

While lecture has enormous potential to inspire and to inform, its capacity to promote the development of higher-order thinking skills, a goal of reform, has been challenged by numerous studies and meta-studies. Costin (1972) examined 58 studies from 1928 to 1967, which compared various aspects of lecture and discussion. Both pedagogies were shown to be equally effective for presenting factual information or for enunciating principles. Pascarella and Terenzini (1991) concluded on the basis of an extensive literature review on class size and productivity that for the accretion of factual knowledge, class size was irrelevant. However, both literature reviews concluded that discussion, particularly small group (15-20) interchanges, had greater potential than lecture for developing skills that require students to integrate knowledge into existing frames of reference and to apply conceptual knowledge to situation-specific problems.

In the traditional classroom, lecture can be enhanced and discussion stimulated by the use of new computer-based technologies. Presentation software such as Powerpoint, Astound, and Wordperfect Presenter can produce text, graphics, video, and animation. Clip-art libraries such as Corel Draw (version 3 and up), Corel Gallery, and Wordperfect are also the source of original graphics and animation to help emphasize important points in the lecture. The Internet, too, is a useful source of graphics and sound files, but creative lecturers need to be aware of copyright issues.

A lecture/demonstration can be enhanced further by computer simulation. For example, to show how a fire sprinkler operates it is usually necessary to go to a special facility, set the sprinkler off and watch the water fall. In the act, the sprinkler is partially destroyed. Therefore, it must be replaced in order to do another demonstration. A computer simulation, on the other hand, offers a number of advantages over traditional presentations: (1) simulations have the characteristics of illustrating or collapsing or expanding time, which can focus students' attention on critical aspects that might be missed and not be repeatable in a live demonstration; (2) simulations can become "educational field trips" that allow students to "visit" sites without the time and expense of travel; and (3) simulations can eliminate risks associated with "real' situations such as operating a commercial boiler or performing a delicate surgical procedure.

A third form of classroom interaction, learner-learner, has

enormous potential to facilitate student learning and to develop career-enhancing social skills (Bonwell and Eison 1991; Johnson, Johnson, and Smith 1991; Moore 1989a). Cooperative learning is a pedagogical strategy designed to give students direct experience with peer teaching, peer learning, motivational feedback, and higher-order thinking. Small groups work together in a structured process to enhance their own and each other's learning and social skills. One study reported measurable improvement in test taking among students working cooperatively in a structured process when compared to individuals working on their own (Lambiotte et al. 1987). Other salutary effects include reduced absenteeism, renewed self-esteem, and improved race relations (Slavin 1983).

Cooperative learning can be facilitated by conferencing software, which is a technical variation of e-mail. As small groups of students work together on a particular project, the professor can monitor and guide each group online. Conferencing software has proven to be a successful classroom stimulus in various disciplines. In English composition class, writing instruction can be enhanced by a focus on process, peer review, and collaboration—all strategies that conferencing software can facilitate.

However, most instructors shy away from integrating cooperative learning into the classroom ecology (with or without the assistance of conferencing software) for any of several reasons, including perceptions that competitiveness and individuality are virtues to be cultivated (which speaks directly to the resilience of core values); that structuring cooperative group process is too difficult to manage; and that students are too immature to work successfully among themselves (Dede 1990). Since most instructors have so little practice with alternative learning strategies, the traditional college classroom is unlikely to change much without a significant institutional investment in professional development.

The Virtual Classroom
Students registering for classes on the virtual campus discover an unprecedented array of learning options made possible by advances in instructional technology and learning theory. The new theory is *constructivism*:

Constructivism is concerned with the process of how we

construct *knowledge. How we construct knowledge depends upon what the learners already know, which depends on the kinds of experiences that they have had, how the learners have organized those experiences into knowledge structures, and the learners' beliefs that are invoked when interpreting events in the world. . . . Constructivist models of learning strive to create environments in ways that are intended to help them construct their own knowledge, rather than having the teacher interpret the world and insure that students understand the world as they have told them* (Jonassen 1995, p. 42–43).

Instead of remaining passive listeners or occasional discussants in a traditional lecture hall, students actively discover and construct their own knowledge. Depending upon the needs of the individual and the resources of the institution, at least eight new learning environments (Tucker 1995b), pioneered by distance learning practitioners, are available today on U.S. college and university campuses:

One-way audio/visual classrooms. Full motion picture and sound are transmitted from a studio location to classrooms on campus or to remote sites, such as home, office, or industrial worksite. Closed circuit educational programs and telecourses delivered by cable or satellite are popular examples of this medium.

Two-way audio/visual classrooms. Popularly known as Interactive Television (ITV), physical classrooms on the same or different campuses are technologically linked for real-time learner-instructor and learner-learner interaction.

Two-way audio classrooms. Live interactive classroom sessions, without the video component, are possible with ordinary telephone transmission technology. An instructor may interact with students at home or in one or more classrooms. Audio-conferencing technology is usually employed to facilitate interaction.

Two-way audio graphic classrooms. Similar to two-way audio, this method permits the visualization of materials otherwise displayed in the traditional classroom on white- or blackboards. "Modern audio graphic systems can do a marginal job using one phone line and a good job with two conditioned lines" (Tucker 1995b, p. 44).

Desktop groupware conferencing. In this modality, instructor and students are linked by personal computers using phone or Internet connections. Sessions can be real time (supplemented by audio with a second phone line) or asynchronous or both.

Desktop video conferencing. Compression technology now permits more advanced computer-mediated conferencing by offering real-time or asynchronous video recording.

Asynchronous desktop conferencing. An exclusively asynchronous modality, this method permits fax storage and retrieval and, in some cases, voice-mail services. "In an important sense, the software is the university" (Tucker 1995bp. 44).

Asynchronous/CD-ROM hybrids. When combined with CD-ROM technology, asynchronous conferencing creates multimedia learning opportunities for students with appropriate computer peripherals. Video, sound, and text supplements, often available as ancillary course material from publishers, add a richness to asynchronous computer-mediated conferencing.

The strategic planning and financial considerations necessary to implement one or more of the available modalities will be discussed later, in section six. At this point, however, it is important to emphasize the essential neutrality of technological environments with respect to learning. Clark (1983) and Russell (1993) independently reviewed several decades of media comparison studies and concluded that instructional media (1) were not inherently superior and (2) did not directly influence student achievement.

The best current evidence is that media are more vehicles that deliver instruction but do not influence student achievement anymore than the truck that delivers our groceries cause change in nutrition. . . . Only the content of the vehicle can influence achievement (Clark 1983, p. 445).

Russell puts a slightly different spin on the findings:

> No matter how it is produced, how it is delivered, whether
> or not it is interactive, low-tech or high-tech, students learn
> equally well with each technology and learn as well as their
> on-campus, face-to-face counterparts even though students
> would rather be on campus with the instructor if that were
> a real choice (1993, p. 2).

Two additional conclusions may be drawn from the summative research of Clark and Russell: (1) Although technology is essentially neutral with respect to learning, the new campus environment made possible by technological innovation creates almost unlimited educational opportunities for students, even those constrained by time and distance factors; and (2) well established methods of instruction—demonstration, simulation, and visualization, for example—may be enhanced by newly available technologies.

Potential for interaction

On the virtual campus, four kinds of interaction are possible: learner-content, learner-instructor, learner-learner, and (unique to the virtual classroom) learner-interface. Learner-content interaction is thought to be enhanced in the virtual classroom because of the variety of ways content can be conveyed electronically—verbally, graphically, and kinesthetically. Learners may interact with content via computer software, CD-ROM, radio and television broadcast, as well as audio- and videotape recordings. One-way communication, such as audio- or videotape, is solely learner-content interactive in nature and therefore demands a high degree of self-direction and independence, qualities especially suited to the adult learner (Knowles 1984).

In the virtual classroom, learner-instructor interaction and learner-learner interaction are problematic considerations. Lacking traditional face-to-face contact, educational success in a virtual environment is critically dependent upon methods of instruction and the ability to exploit characteristics of available technologies. While it is possible to learn much through learner-content interaction, it is through the complex, recursive social process of instruction that individually acquired knowledge obtains validation. Shale (1988) further explains:

On the virtual campus, four kinds of interaction are possible: learner-content, learner-instructor, learner-learner, and (unique to the virtual classroom) learner-interface.

A defining characteristic of education is that it is a process of validating private knowledge, and a process of recurring validation of what has previously come to be known through education. In order to validate what one knows, one has to hold such knowledge up for public inspection by other people who have received public recognition as "knowers" in the particular field of interest (p. 2).

From simply confirming facts to negotiating the meaning of difficult concepts and their interrelationships, social interaction is an important pedagogical tool in both traditional and virtual classroom instruction.

Distance learning theorists and practitioners, ever conscious of mainstream detractors, are sensitive to the issue of social interaction. In the traditional classroom, teacher/student interaction isaeffected by methods designed for that purpose: intense discussion as well as active and cooperative learning techniques. In the electronic classroom, the choice of modality will influence how interaction will be conducted. For instance, with desktop groupware conferencing, teacher/student interaction may take place in real time, asynchronously, or both. Tucker (1995b) suggests one advantage to asynchronous interaction—more considered deliberation and response. Given the predominance of lecture in traditional venues, it is no wonder that Shale can ironically note that distance learning modalities offer opportunities for making learning more personal.

Learner-learner interaction in the virtual classroom can be conducted in real time or asynchronously. Audio, video, and computer conferencing permit a degree of real-time interaction not previously available in conventional distance learning scenarios (Barker, Frisbie and Patrick 1989). Research findings on cooperative learning in the virtual classroom are similar to those for traditional classrooms (Gallini and Helms 1993; Riel 1994; Spaulding and Lake 1991). When students work together with well-defined goals and clear accountability guidelines, a number of benefits accrue: increased self-esteem, improved academic and social skills, and reduction of ethnic tension (Sharon 1984; Slavin 1985).

Opportunities for international cooperative learning experiences are greatly enhanced by breakthroughs in compression technology, such as Cornell University's CU-See-Me software, which permits videoconferencing via the Internet (Barker 1994). Electronic mail and network bulletin boards continue to make possible asynchronous interaction, such as thoughtful and provocative responses to prior real-time discussions. This ability to address complex international issues, within varying social, cultural, and political contexts, offers students a unique opportunity to cooperate in a global environment. Instructors, however, need to refrain from monopolizing the discussion or making presentations that other technologies (such as print or videotape) could more appropriately supply (Moore 1989b). Learner-learner interaction can and should become an integral part of instructional course design for the virtual classroom.

A fourth type of interaction must be accommodated in the virtual classroom: learner-interface, that is, the interaction that occurs between the learner and the various technologies a particular institution may provide for the delivery of instruction (Hillman, Willis and Gunawardena 1994). Instructional technology should possess functional simplicity, and when that technology does not, it has a negative impact on learning (Schrum 1992). Hillman, Willis, and Gunawardena (1994) define learner-interface interaction as "a process of manipulating tools to accomplish a task" (p. 34). Instructional program design should include opportunities for students to "become comfortable with the interface, accepting of the technology and, consequently, comfortable with and accepting of the content of the instruction" (p. 36). The authors further suggest that, for purposes of our virtual classroom, students become acclimated to the appropriate technologies by way of technology credit courses, orientation sessions, and in-class exercises (p. 36).

Interface Capabilities
The interface, or point of interaction between the learner and the technology, becomes a window or a gateway to a variety of intellectually challenging activities. The technology itself, such as multimedia or hypertext, does not teach; it is, however, the vehicle for instruction set by the curriculum. Classroom reform, for the purpose of meeting individual needs and promoting constructivist models of learning, is predicated on curriculum reform. For present purposes, curriculum may be defined as "an intentional design for learning negotiated by faculty in light of their specialized

knowledge and in the context of social expectations and students' needs" (Toombs and Tierney 1991, p. 21). The significance of this definition lies in its emphasis on contextual considerations: a *particular* faculty addressing the needs of a *particular* student body at a *particular* institution. Faculty judgment is the crucial factor here; what works as an instructional strategy in one situation does not of necessity work for another. Too often in the past a potentially enabling technology has been acquired by administration, made available for classroom use, and subsequently ignored by those best able to ascertain its instructional value, the classroom instructor.

When faculty participate in the selection of modalities that will carry the content and facilitate interaction, "they knowingly or unknowingly are curriculum developers" (Means et al. 1993, p. 67). As a process, curriculum design identifies a problem and formulates a solution. A major faculty responsibility on the virtual campus is staying abreast of software solutions to curriculum problems. For example, the eight new learning environments identified earlier in this section are *communication* technologies, which in most instances are made possible by powerful interactive software. Computer software—the instructions or programs that reside in a computer's memory—can be divided into two groups: *tutorial* and *exploratory.*

Tutorial

Computer software performs a *tutorial* function when it provides students with opportunities for *demonstration* and *practice* (Means et al. 1993).

Demonstrations, which visually display phenomena, have been used for centuries to enhance instruction. Today, the truism "A picture is worth a thousand words" has been updated by computer animation techniques and graphic capabilities to read: "A moving picture is worth a million words." In the virtual classroom dynamic mathematical concepts and processes are rendered visually, in some cases for the first time (Zimmerman and Cunningham 1991); art students generate rough designs for subsequent sculptures and castings (Mones-Hattal et a.l 1990); and ophthalmology residents observe the origins and development of ocular disease (Brown 1991).

Practice refers to drill and practice, a traditional, behaviorist approach to learning in which computer software provides the learner with step-by-step instruction (Thompson, Simonson and Hargrave 1992). Computer Assisted Instruction (CAI) dates to the 1960s when Patrick Suppes and Richard Atkinson of Stanford University developed computer programs for math and reading that featured learner feedback and gradual escalation in content and levels of difficulty based upon prior performance (Coburn et al. 1982).

Intelligent CAI, or Intelligent Tutoring Systems (ITS), provide a promising alternative to traditional CAI. Like CAI, intelligent CAI makes adjustments in degree of difficulty and complexity; however, intelligent CAI bases its estimations not on past student performance but on inferences or models of student knowledge and understanding (Sleeman and Brown 1982).

Exploratory

Computer software also furnishes students the opportunity to explore facts, ideas, and complex simulated environments for self-directed learning. Two such exploratory domains are *electronic databases* and *microworlds* (Means et al 1993).

On-line computer *databases* have experienced phenomenal growth in each of the last two decades. Early on, library microcomputers were used extensively to search remote bibliographic databases such as DIALOG and Orbit. CD-ROM technology, with its user-friendly interface and fixed-cost usage, became the vehicle of choice for reference libraries and patrons (Silberger 1995). Today, virtual classroom students, remotely situated but with microcomputer and modem within fingertip reach, access Online Public Access Catalogs (OPACs), which have replaced traditional card catalogs at their college or university library (Sudweks, Collins, and December 1995). Enterprising students can access and interactively search several hundred OPACs as well as remote archives via the Internet (Ellsworth 1995). The virtue of such access is that learners can explore at their own pace and level of proficiency virtually any topic in any form (i.e., text, pictures, animation, film clips, and statistics) (Santoro 1995). In addition, programs such as Project Gutenberg at St. Augustine College, Oxford Text Archive, and the National Center for Machine-Readable Texts at Princeton University are making available on-line full-text journal articles and books for instantaneous reading and reference use (Tomer 1992).

A *microworld* is another exploratory domain that expanded computing power has made possible. A typical microworld builds upon both traditional and computer-generated visualization techniques to create a simulated environment in which the learner acts and reacts to unfolding events within a prestructured scenario (Dede 1987). Simulations have been widely used for years to provide personnel training in government, private industry, and the military (Auld and Pantelidis 1994). As an active, classroom learning experience, participants express feelings, make choices, communicate with partners, and manipulate objects: "[K]nowledge is not just a copy of reality. To know an object or an event does not mean that one simply looks at it and makes an image or mental copy of it. To know something involves action on it. Thus, operation, an internalized action is the essence of knowledge" (Diulus and Baum 1991).

Progress on issues and problem-solving are usually dependent upon interpersonal communication. Participants seek a consensus of agreement on an issue. There is a double-edged element during negotiations between competition and cooperation. A player wants to advance one's self interests while realizing that compromise is often necessary (p. 36).

Summary

Systemic reform has brought about a number of changes to postsecondary education, none more significant than what students learn and how they learn it. With time and distance effectively removed as constraints, colleges and universities are serving a more heterogeneous clientele with diverse educational backgrounds and needs. As Plater suggests, "these new century students confront us with the possibility that postsecondary educational systems designed to manage enrollment growth by weeding out unprepared or uncommitted students may no longer be appropriate or economically defensible" (p. 9). If one major goal is to cultivate an expert work force for the Information Age, then postsecondary education will have to accommodate a range of skills and aptitudes.

Perhaps the most telling difference between learning in the traditional and virtual modes is the kind and extent of interaction. In the traditional classroom, the potential for learner-instructor and learner-learner interaction is very high, but instructors have largely ignored this mandate for change and continue to employ the lecture mode as the predominant method of instruction.

> *Such a lack of concern about the quality of teaching stems from the "tyranny of proximity," a frame of mind in which important issues are overlooked because they are so much an accepted part of day-to-day activities that they remain unquestioned and unchallenged. Partly as a consequence of such a mindset, there has been no significant qualitative change in approaches to teaching in conventional higher education institutions for at least the past 100 years* (Taylor 1994, p. 179).

In the virtual classroom, on the other hand, technology supports collaborative learning, heterogeneous groupings, problem-solving and higher-order thinking skills—educational processesthat a lecture format cannot facilitate. Dede (1990) suggests other fundamental differences with electronic interaction:

With time and distance effectively removed as constraints, colleges and universities are serving a more heterogeneous clientele with diverse educational backgrounds and needs.

1. *Information technologies are predominantly a visual medium, rather than the textual and auditory environment of the conventional classroom.*
2. *The affective content of technology-mediated messages is muted compared to face-to-face interaction.*
3. *Complex cognitive content can be conveyed more readily in electronic form because multiple representations of material (e.g., animations, text, verbal descriptions, visual images) can be presented to give learners many ways of understanding the fundamental concept* (pp. 258-59).

For institutions involved in distance education, the opportunities to explore the capabilities of these new technologies in both traditional and virtual learning environments may yet yield solutions to vexing problems in teaching and learning. Following an institutional commitment to professional development, traditional and virtual teaching and learning can and should complement one another in the search for educational excellence.

RESEARCH AND THE NEW SCHOLARLY AGENDA

American universities are products of the late 19th and early 20th centuries. The question is, how do you break them up in some way, at least get some group of young people who are free of them? How do you make them free to do something new and different? Everett Hughes (quoted by Schon 1995, p. 34)

On the virtual campus both the nature of research and the role of the scholar are the subjects of renewed interest and intense debate. "It is a battle of snails," contends Donald Schon, "proceeding so slowly that you have to look very carefully in order to see it going on. But it is happening nonetheless" (1995, p. 32). At stake is how research and scholarly endeavors will be conducted on college campuses in this Age of Information. The debate focuses on four separate but ultimately interconnected issues: (1) Are colleges and universities responding effectively to societal demands for greater balance between the teaching, research, and service functions? (2) Can the definition of scholarship be expanded to accommodate the demand for greater emphasis on the teaching and service functions? (3) How is information technology transforming research? and (4) Do different forms of scholarly activity require new epistemologies? The resolution of these and similar issues is likely to shape the agenda for research and scholarship for years to come.

Scholarly Tradition and Societal Trends

The history of scholarly activity at American colleges and universities is one of continuous forming and reforming (Boyer 1990; Parsons and Platt 1973; Rudolph 1990; Shils 1978; Veysey 1970). For more than 350 years, since the founding of Harvard College in 1636, three functions— teaching, service, and research— have, by turns, shaped the ethos of higher education institutions (Bowen 1980).

The role of faculty at the colonial college was generally restricted to promoting the intellectual, moral, and spiritual development of students preparing for the ministry. Teaching was considered a vocation as well, and those "called" to teach, according to historian Theodore Benditt, "were hired [by colleges] not for their scholarly ability or achievement but for their religious commitment. Scholarly achievement was not a high priority, either for professors or students" (quoted by Boyer 1990, p. 4). The more serious and productive scholarship—in the modern sense—took place outside and away from colonial colleges. Amateur scientists and scholars, lacking intellectual communities, never quite achieved results as significant as their European contemporaries, yet remained the dominant intellectual force in America until scholarship became institutionalized later in the universities (Shils 1978).

Although the tradition of university scholar as teacher and mentor persisted well into the nineteenth century, the foundation was being laid for the addition of a second scholarly function. As Boyer (1990) explains, "A new country was being formed and higher education's focus began to shift from the shaping of young lives to the building of a nation" (p. 4). *Service* was added to the mission of private and public universities, particularly land grant colleges, with the passage of the Morrill Act of 1862, which gave federal land to states for the purpose of funding both liberal arts and technical education, and the Hatch Act of 1887, which created agricultural experiment stations that brought technical forms of higher education to the midwest and prairie states. The technical training that students acquired at land grant institutions would eventually "undergird the emerging agricultural and mechanical revolution" (Boyer 1990, p. 5). While the idea of education as serving a democratic function became firmly rooted during this period, "a new faculty orientation towards applied research was born, defining in another unique way the future American research university" (Katz 1993, p. 14).

Basic research at American universities came in response to a set of circumstances that materialized between the end of the Civil War and the conclusion of World War I (Shils 1978). First of all, the universities were the ideal locus for the discovery and diffusion of knowledge in part because their main rivals, amateur scholars and scientists and later independent research institutions, could not sustain the requisite drain on resources nor duplicate the intellectual milieu found on bustling university campuses. Funding for university instruction, ironically, served as the economic foundation for early research projects. After teaching rounds were completed, professors made time for original research, motivated almost solely by intellectual curiosity. Furthermore,

> *It was a time when the financial requirements for research were not large. There were few large-scale pro-*

*jects for which many assistants had to be used. Much
research was conducted by single teachers, sometimes
by a teacher and one of his pupils. The equipment,
which was seldom very elaborate, did not cost much
and a good part of it could be paid for from the costs of
maintaining the laboratories needed for teaching* (Shils
1978, p. 168).

While the center of campus activity remained undergraduate
education, infused by the Scottish model of regularized curriculum, basic research in the fledgling sciences took shape,
if only on the periphery of academic life.

Shortly after the Civil War, young Americans returning
from German universities began to clamor for a more sophisticated academic model. The focus of the complaint was
the lack of institutional structure and reward system necessary to stimulate a shift in ethos from a purely pedagogical
orientation to one emphasizing scholarly and scientific research. Altbach (1992) describes the origins and impact the
German university research model had upon American
higher education institutions:

*In the mid-nineteenth century, a newly united Germany
harnessed the university for nation-building. Under the
leadership of Wilhelm von Humboldt, German higher
education was given significant resources by the state,
took on the responsibility for research aimed at national
development and industrialization, and played a key
role in defining the ideology of the new German nation.
The reformed German universities also established graduate education and the doctoral degree as a major focus
of the institution. Research became for the first time an
integral function of the university. The university was
recognized as a hierarchy based upon the newly emerging scientific disciplines. American reformers took these
German innovations and further transformed higher
education by stressing the links between the university
and society through the concept of service and direct
relationships with industry and agriculture, democra-
tized the German chair system through the establishment of academic departments and the development of
the "land grant" concept for both high-level research
and expanded access to higher education"* (p. 41).

The German influence was palpable, but it was not until the establishment of postgraduate studies at a handful of institutions that a paradigm shift of the first order occurred (Veysey 1970). With the founding of the Johns Hopkins University in 1876—in Shils's estimation, "the most decisive single event in the history of learning in the Western hemisphere" (1978, p. 171)—and subsequently Clark University in 1887 and the University of Chicago in 1892, American universities began a shift in ethos, subtly at first, from values that espoused the distribution of inherited knowledge to ones that encouraged the creation of new knowledge. Teaching was still regarded as a primary mission, but scholarly research now attained a position of unprecedented importance.

Not all American universities responded to the pull of research. Over time, a marked division of labor occurred between universities that supported both teaching and research and liberal arts colleges that sought to maintain traditional values. Even within research institutions, a division of labor occurred between younger faculty who taught elementary classes and senior faculty who taught the more advanced, research-oriented ones (Shils 1978).

The Second World War and its aftermath brought additional modification to the nature and scope of scholarly endeavor. For the first time federal support for research was initiated as part of an effort to bring the war to a rapid and successful conclusion (Boyer 1990). The Office of Scientific Research and Development was founded in 1940, bringing academic talent to Washington and grant money to university campuses. This wartime collaboration of university talent and federal bureaucracy opened the doors to postwar federal support for university research.

Despite profound societal changes in the half century following World War II, no corresponding paradigmatic shift in scholarly activity has taken place. The dramatic expansion of postsecondary education did indeed produce, in Trow's description, a transformation from an *elite* to a *mass* to a *universal* system of higher education (Altback 1992). Furthermore, the demands from industry for graduates with specialized training did produce a greater variety of course and program options at comprehensive universities. However, as Lynton (1984) argues, higher education continues to face a "disturbing paradox":

The university sector has expanded in response to external *needs: the baby boom and the growing societal
demand for skilled professionals in an expanding
number of fields. But the essential center of the university continues to be driven by* internal *values and priorities that have changed little or not at all from those
that prevailed before the war under quite different
circumstances* (p. 64).

More recent technological, economic, demographic, and
political trends, cited at the outset of this monograph, have
put enormous pressure on colleges and universities to reform from within. Yet, with respect to scholarly activity,
college faculty nationwide report on survey after survey that
the pressure to publish research not only remains the key
requirement for tenure but a major inhibitor to improved
teaching (Boyer 1992; Daly 1994).

A Reconceptualization of Scholarship
Signs of renewed interest in the nature of research and the
role of the scholar may be found in academy journals, business publications, and government reports (Boyer 1990;
Carnevale et al. 1990, 1991; Daly 1994; Lynton and Elman
1987; Paulsen and Feldman 1995; Rice and Richlin 1993).
Calls for a redistribution of faculty work, aimed at placing
greater emphasis on undergraduate teaching, have stirred a
debate over the value and meaning of scholarship and of
the relationship between teaching and research.

The value of empirical research
Critics of higher education who contend that college faculty
spend disproportionate time on research, to the detriment of
undergraduate teaching, can point to reports deriving from
statistics compiled by the Institute for Scientific Information
(Daly 1994).

*One such report estimated that, of all the articles pub-
lished in even the most prestigious natural and social
science journals, less than one-half were ever cited by
anyone, that less than one-fifth were cited more than
once, and that many of the meager number of citations
that were garnered were the result of self-citations by
the authors in subsequent publications of their own.*

These data raise the ugly possibility that much of the
published research the professorate has felt itself com-
pelled to generate has never been read, or at least cited,
by anyone—not even by other specialists working in the
same fields in which it is published (Daly 1994, p. 47).

On the other hand, proponents of the status quo argue
persuasively that American universities "will not be able to
attract, hold and properly support the work of first-rate
scholars if they must impose heavy teaching responsibilities
on them" (Daly 1994, p. 49).

Using Nobel Prizes as one measure of the contributions to
fundamental human knowledge, American researchers since
1945 account for more than half of the Prizes awarded in
physics, chemistry, and medicine; before 1945, they had
garnered just 18 of 129 (Boyer 1990). Proponents contend
that such advances could be seriously jeopardized if the
research is curtailed in favor of competing obligations.

Other de facto circumstances mitigate against reform of
the research function. For instance, the current organization
of colleges and universities clearly reflect a research orientation (Altbach 1992; Daly 1994; Shils 1978). The formation
and institutionalization of autonomous academic
departments have given a sense of collective identity to
scholars and have nurtured their development (Shils 1978).
Reconfiguring departments for purposes of greater interdisciplinary cooperation is salutary in theory, but difficult in practice to achieve. Furthermore, the well-established reward
system, which faculty surveys acknowledge is stronger than
ever, has produced a culture of scholarship that has trickled
down from America's preeminent research institutions to cast
"a shadow over the entire higher learning enterprise" (Boyer
1990, p. 12), including comprehensive universities and liberal arts and community colleges. Expecting to alter the behavior of scholars at all kinds of institutions in the absence
of a comparable reward structure seems unrealistic at best.

Scholarship and teaching

Another aspect of the debate concerning the nature of scholarship is its purported relationship to college teaching.
Restoring balance between these two major functions of a
college faculty—research and teaching—has been at the
center of a longstanding philosophical debate over the very

idea of higher education or, more precisely, the idea of a university. On the one hand, we have the historical alignment of Jaspers, Griffith, and Wagener who included research as part of the definition of a university (Barnett 1992). On a pedagogical level, most faculty today express in surveys the belief that research enhances teaching (Centra 1983). One survey by Jauch (1976) in particular reported that 95 percent of natural science faculty and department heads at one college believed that research actually increases classroom effectiveness "by increasing awareness and currency" (Centra 1983, p. 379).

On the other hand, we have the tradition of Newman, Ortega y Gasset, and Sir Walter Moberly arguing that the university "need not or, indeed, should not engage in research. . . [for] knowledge in the context of discovery and knowledge in the context of transmission are entirely different enterprises" (Barnett 1992, p. 620-623). The majority of contemporary scholarly studies, in fact, support the contention that "teaching and research are independent functions, with performance in one unrelated to the other" (Centra 1983, p. 380). Barnett ironically notes that no debate exists over the influence of teaching on research: "research is seldom driven by curricular considerations but is normally given direction by an interest structure based on academic careers and the public use of knowledge" (1992, p. 623).

Reconfiguring departments for purposes of greater interdisciplinary cooperation is salutary in theory, but difficult in practice to achieve.

"Aggregative" scholarship

The debate over the relative importance of research and teaching and the relationship between the two is unlikely to be resolved soon. In the interim, Daly (1994) proposes a kind of "aggregative" scholarship as a bridge between scholarship and teaching. By expanding the definition of scholarship—and the reward system that supports it—scholars will be free to address a much wider audience for their publications. Aggregative scholarship means selecting, analyzing, interpreting, and summarizing the most important and up-to-date research finding in one's field, presented in nonspecialist's language, for other faculty members who wish to keep up with advances in other fields, for public school teachers who need to keep abreast of changes in their subject specialties, and for members of the business community who want to explore the commercial possibilities of new research findings.

Daly (1994) cites three advantages to aggregative scholarship. First, "it should impact directly and beneficially on undergraduate teaching" (p. 51). As recipients of such information, hard-pressed faculty members would be able to continue their specialized research while remaining up-to-date on advances elsewhere. The classroom payoff would be lectures presented and discussions moderated by well-versed instructors.

Second, "unlike research on pedagogy, the shift in standards necessary to legitimize aggregative scholarship would be a relatively small one— both for college faculty themselves and for the journal editors and personnel committees who judge their work" (Daly 1994, p. 53). That is, aggregative scholars need not become expert in pedagogical theory but will broadly communicate the findings in their own fields. Daly cites examples of scholars who became "popularizers" of their disciplines without suffering the loss of scholarly respectability: Stephen J. Gould, life sciences; Jacob Bronowski, mathematics; John Kenneth Galbraith, economics; and Carl Sagan, astronomy.

Finally, such scholarship "could help to make the economic case for higher education by making a direct contribution in two areas that have already been identified as central to the rebuilding of the American economy—the strengthening of competence and morale among public school teachers and the capacity for innovation in the American business community" (Daly 1994, p. 53). Factors making the publication of aggregative scholarship particularly beneficial to public school teachers include inadequate professional development, out-of-date textbooks, and infrequently taught subjects. Within the business community, such publications would assist decisionmakers to extract from specialized research the information necessary to remain commercially competitive.

Daly (1994) concludes his proposal by reminding members of the academy that teaching and research, two vital faculty functions, are currently in a state of disequilibrium: "The elevation of aggregative scholarship to scholarly respectability, however, could help to restore the balance between the two to a state of healthy equilibrium" (p. 55).

"Enlarging the perspective"
In recent years, many faculty and administrators have added their voices to the debate by calling for an expanded view

of scholarship that, in the view of Paulsen and Feldman (1995), "encompasses and encourages the full range of diverse, creative talents of faculty, allows for different disciplinary perspectives, and provides a framework for the development of mission statements expressing more distinctive and differentiated priorities" (p. 615).

Perhaps the most influential voice confronting the research monolith comes from the Carnegie Foundation for the Advancement of Teaching. In *Scholarship Reconsidered,* Boyer (1990) proposes a four-dimensional model of scholarship, each element separate yet interdependent: the scholarship of *discovery;* the scholarship of *integration;* the scholarship of *application;* and the scholarship of *teaching.* Paulsen and Feldman (1995) report that Boyer's proposal has already been adopted by the National Project on Institutional Priorities and Faculty Rewards for the purpose of promoting the reconceptualization of scholarship among various academic disciplines.

The first element of the model, the *scholarship of discovery,* consolidates graduate training with the research function. "The processes of research and discovery lead to the creation and advancement of knowledge, and expand the capacity to make meaning out of existing knowledge" (Paulsen and Feldman 1995, p. 623). Traditionally, the rite of passage is the doctoral dissertation, which "offers definitive proof of students' knowledge of their disciplines, ability to engage in independent research, and ability to present findings in a coherent manner" (Hamilton 1990, p. 47). In many disciplines, the dissertation represents a "new beginning" after years of coursework, examinations, and trial scholarship—class papers, research projects, masters' theses. As an integral part of doctoral education, the traditional dissertation constitutes, in theory, a significant and original contribution to knowledge. However, as one dean who participated in the Council of Graduate Schools study on *The Role and Nature of the Doctoral Dissertation* noted pithily, "What is original may not be significant and what is significant may not be original" (quoted in Richlin 1993, p. 51).

The dean's comment underscores a set of problems associated with training tomorrow's scholars and researchers: "Although many faculty and others see the dissertation as a sacred institution, not to be tampered with, other members of the graduate education community increasingly agree that parts of the process, as well as many of the final products, may be out of step with the academic enterprise and, indeed, with society's overall intellectual and research needs" (Hamilton 1990, p. 47).

Among already-established university researchers, the current system of tenure and promotion necessitates the implementation of fairly rigid timetables for launching research projects and publishing results. In a 1990 survey of chief academic officers on the relative importance among teaching, research, and service, Miller (1995) reports that more than a quarter observed their institutions moving toward research and away from teaching and service. The trend was even more pronounced at doctoral institutions, where 56 percent observed the same movement (Boyer 1990). In the prevailing milieu, it is no wonder that so many faculty believe that their publications "were merely counted, never read" by those making personnel recommendations (Daly 1994, p. 47).

On an optimistic note, *Campus Trends 1995* (El-Khawas 1995) reports that many institutions are just now beginning to respond positively to Boyer's call for more balance among the teaching, research, and service functions. In El-Khawas's annual survey of over 500 colleges and universities,

> *Close to half have increased the importance of teaching in faculty evaluations. Among public research and doctoral universities, two-thirds reported such changes. About four in ten institutions now give greater importance to teaching in their hiring decisions. One-third have made changes in the criteria for promotion of faculty. About three in ten have changed the criteria for tenure. Among public research and doctoral universities, six in ten reported such changes* (p. 20).

Few institutions, however, have begun to organize faculty service initiatives, leaving such activities to the discretion of individual faculty members. The notable exceptions are treatment centers and technical institutes found on the campuses of the larger public universities (El Khawas 1995, p. 20).

As Boyer has acknowledged, the university research establishment has a rich and proud heritage of achievement by any standard of measurement. Restoring balance among faculty functions, however, will go far in affirming the diversity and creativity of college faculty, not all of whom need or should be wholly absorbed in searching for new facts or creating new knowledge and theory.

The second element of the model, the *scholarship of integration,* means "making connections across the disciplines, placing the specialties in larger context, illuminating data in a revealing way, often educating nonspecialists, too " (Boyer 1990, p. 18). The scholarship of integration has implications for the conduct of research and for the practice of teaching. As a focus of research, integration includes *interpretation,* "filtering one's own research—or the research of others—into larger intellectual patterns" (p. 17). Since the growth of specialization, particularly after the Second World War, scholars have produced mountains of new data within specific disciplines. The concern remains that an accelerating "publish or perish" mindset will encourage the production of unextrapolated data or, worse yet, reduce scholarship to pedantry. In addition, the scholarship of integration promotes *interdisciplinary* initiatives. Interaction among representatives of various disciplines has as its purpose the generation of new conceptual models of our knowledge structure as well as an understanding of the roles specific disciplines play in that creation.

The scholarship of integration has implications for the practice of teaching as well. Typically, a student registers for prerequisites, requisites, and electives spanning a variety of disciplines. Possible and even appropriate connections among disciplines are not usually made by the course instructor; whatever synthesis does occur, the student makes. However, faculty engaged in the scholarship of integration are perhaps ideal candidates to develop and implement integrative teaching techniques. A scholarship of integration can be nurtured, at least in part, by redirecting institutional rewards to encourage scholars, in their research and in their teaching, to continually shape and reshape the boundaries of human knowledge.

The next element of the model, the *scholarship of application,* "moves toward engagement as the scholar asks, 'How can knowledge be responsibly applied to consequential problems? How can it be helpful to individuals as well as institutions?' And further, 'Can social problems *themselves* define an agenda for scholarly investigation?'" (Boyer 1990, p. 23).

In linking theory with practice for the purpose of applying knowledge to solve society's problems, American colleges and universities are at the center of a historic paradox.

On the one hand, American higher education institutions, particularly land grant colleges, have a long-standing commitment to social service. The agricultural and mechanical revolutions of the nineteenth century owe much of their momentum to the utilitarian mission of these institutions. On the other hand, "the scholarship of practice lost its pragmatic roots when the professional schools became part of the university and adopted the academy's emphasis on science" (Richlin 1993, p. 44). It has been argued that the 1910 Flexner report on medical education did much to dichotomize theory and practice, by separating knowledge into hierarchical stages—theory and research at the top, clinical practice at the bottom (Rice and Richlin 1993). Following the lead of medicine, many other professions such as law, engineering, and dentistry followed suit with their own versions of the Flexner report and instituted academic reform that put increasing emphasis on the basic scientific component.

A modern scholarship of application requires first and foremost an indication of parameters. "To be considered *scholarship,* service activities must be tied directly to one's special field of knowledge and relate to, and flow directly out of, this professional activity. Such service is serious, demanding work, requiring the rigor—and the accountability—traditionally associated with research activities" (Boyer 1990, p. 22). Professional service might include, but is not restricted to, "technical consulting, evaluation and policy analysis, scholarly writing for the nonspecialists, technology transfer mechanisms, and related extension activities" (Paulsen and Feldman 1995, p. 625). Furthermore, service must be distinguished from *citizenship.* Campus activities, such as sitting on committees or advising student organizations, and civic activities, such as charitable work, should be encouraged but not confused with scholarship.

Unlike the German university paradigm, where knowledge is an end in itself, the American university has the opportunity to confront its own history and fulfill one of its traditional missions by putting the needs of a pragmatic society on an equal footing with the scholarship of discovery. "This enlarged view of scholarship," Rice and Richlin conclude, "if taken seriously, promises to make tomorrow's professoriate more responsive to the shifting scholarly needs of society" (1993, p. 77).

The final element of the four-dimensional model is the *scholarship of teaching*. For community and liberal arts colleges and, in many instances, comprehensive universities, teaching remains today the central mission. Even research institutions are beginning to address the ethical—not to mention the political—dilemma that arises when the education of large numbers of well-prepared undergraduate students is entrusted, at least initially, to graduate student teaching assistants (TAs).

As the stock of teaching rises, so too do the opportunities to elevate teaching to a level of serious scholarship. For many years Cross has promoted the role of "*classroom researcher*— one who is involved in the evaluation of his or her own teaching and learning, even as it takes place. Such a person should be trained to be a careful observer of the teaching process, to collect feedback on what and how well students learn, and to evaluate the effectiveness of instruction" (Boyer 1990, p. 61). Boyer suggests that at community colleges, faculty so inclined might benefit from using a research model to evaluate and improve their own teaching. "We still have much to understand about how students learn, especially those from less advantaged backgrounds, and faculty in community colleges should be authorities on this task" (p. 61).

At liberal arts colleges, where teaching undergraduates remains the raison d'être, the reward structure should support both the scholarship of teaching and integration. Interdisciplinary research and teaching play an important role in creating the ideal learning environments espoused by such institutions.

Research universities as well need to expand their definitions of scholarship if not their missions as institutions. As one doctorate-granting university president put it, "This campus should be a place where great teachers *and* great researchers function side by side. We should have the confidence to say, 'Look, you're a great researcher and we are eager to have you here doing what you do best.' We should also be able to say to a colleague, 'You are terrific with students, but you are not publishing. Still we want you to help us perform an important mission on the campus'" (Boyer 1990, p. 59). Restructuring the definition and scope of scholarly activity to include great teaching reaffirms the centrality of undergraduate education even at "research" institutions.

Although there is a large body of existing pedagogical

research, Rice (1991) has suggested that a fresh dialogue on the scholarship of teaching ought to begin anew. The teaching-learning process is of such complexity and significance as to warrant the scholarly attention of our most able theorists and practitioners. Previously, improvement in teaching was effected in isolation and by trial and error.

Clearly there is an emerging national recognition of the importance of good teaching in postsecondary education. Elevating the scholarship of teaching—and the scholarships of integration and application—to the level of discovery will assist in restoring the balance between the historic trio of faculty activities—teaching, research, and service. If "our entire higher education culture is based upon the presumption of faculty prerogative," as Doucette (1993, p. 53) asserts, then it must be faculty in concert with administration who reengineer the fundamental changes that the various social and economic forces at work in society will otherwise soon mandate.

Online Scholarly Communication and Collaboration

New computer-based technologies become important tools in the reform of traditional scholarship. The relative ease with which scholars today can obtain information and communicate with colleagues is paving the way for proposed new forms of scholarship, such as those promoted by the Carnegie Foundation for the Advancement of Teaching. The Internet and World Wide Web (WWW), in particular, promise, in Harnad's words, to "substantially restructure the pursuit of knowledge" (1990, p. 342).

The Internet, a collection of networks that spans the globe, functions as the backbone for today's online scholarly communication and collaboration. The World Wide Web, a hypertext-based document retrieval system on Unix-based machines linked to the Internet, has become the most popular Internet network. Furthermore, an Internet II has been proposed for the national research community, in part to exploit more fully broadband network capabilities and, in part, to mitigate some of the negative impact that privatization and commercialization have produced on the network systems (Roberts 1996).

Electronic global interactivity has salutary implications for the scholarship of teaching, discovery, integration, and application. The scholarship of teaching, for example, has greatly benefited from the explosive growth and development of the World Wide Web. If prenetwork scholarship was characterized by spatial-temporal and economic constraints, today's scholarship of teaching—courtesy of the WWW—is characterized by unprecedented access to expertise in content and curriculum design, evaluation methodology, graphics and visual communications, cognitive and behavioral psychology, computer programming, and marketing.

A number of WWW homepages have been constructed for the sole purpose of brokering information on curriculum development. SunSITE (www.sunsite.queensu.ca/localov/overview.html) *(Accessed June 30, 1997)*, for example, has proposed a series of initiatives aimed at developing and promoting new educational technologies that can be proven to serve real learning needs in a realistic educational context. Queens University, the sponsor of SunSITE, believes that "the future success of the new technologies will depend upon whether they can be applied easily and cheaply by typical professors teaching typical students, not just by a small band of enthusiasts to a small and selective group of students under highly artificial (and costly) conditions" (p. 1). To that end, SunSITE is developing and maintaining Web pages that will include an online international database of contacts to curriculum designers; annotated directory of existing resources (Web sites, listservs, newsgroups, etc.) related to educational technology; a global conference calendar listing workshops, seminars, and conferences on curriculum development; and electronic workshops with "guest speakers" mediated with interactive videoconferncing software.

Other very valuable resources for teachers and educational researchers are the information clearinghouses for courseware for higher education on the WWW. Courseware may be defined simply as the sum of the content and the electronic vehicles used to convey content, including course syllabi, assignments, class calendars, lecture notes, exams, and interactive products (commercial or shareware). The World Lecture Hall at the University of Texas (www.utexas.edu/world/lecture) *(Accessed June 30, 1997)* is one such clearinghouse, making available hundreds of links to homepages created by faculty delivering courses or class materials on the WWW. Intriguing illustrations, Web courses, or materials include *The Electronic Renaissance* from Boise State University, the *Virtual Media Lab* from the University of Pennsylvania,

WWW—is character- ized by unprece- dented access to expertise in content and curriculum design, evaluation method- ology, graphics and visual communi- cations, cognitive and behavioral psychology, computer program- ming, and marketing.

Multimedia Textbooks from the Virtual Hospital at the University of Iowa, and *Hypertext Supreme Court Cases* from Cornell University. *(Accessed June 30, 1997.)*

The scholarship of discovery—and to a lesser extent the scholarships of integration and application—is on the doorstep of a major revolution. Constrained only by old ways of thinking about publication and scientific communication, scientists today can communicate and collaborate via the Internet with a speed, scope, and scale that no previous methods could ever come close to providing. Extending a basic area of knowledge for the purpose of extending the frontiers of a field begins of necessity with the "prepublication phase of scientific inquiry where most of the cognitive work is done" (Harnad 1990, p. 342). This phase often commences with a literature review, consistent with available university resources. Previous researchers would travel to the campus library during posted hours and manually search for hard-copy documents arranged alpha-numerically on wooden or metal shelves. On the virtual campus, the retrieval power of Online Public Access Catalogs (OPACs), with their Boolean capabilities and various search engines, not only eliminates spatial-temporal constraints but encourages creative new searches of traditional sources (Tomer 1992). Furthermore, the costs associated with the purchase and storage of commercially distributed print books and journals are greatly reduced as electronic journals gain ascendancy.

Internet now empowers scholars to use remote library OPACs on an interactive basis and to transfer documents from distant repositories to the scholar's own microcomputer (Silberger 1995). Telnet, an interactive computer program, provides the capability of generating a customized bibliography of national or international scholarship. "To some degree the availability of OPACs throughout the world is providing an alternative to the expensive, commercially produced remote online bibliographic database systems" (Silberger 1995, p. 105). Meanwhile, to transfer documents either from or to a remote network resource, a scholar employs an FTP (file transfer protocol) program. One application has scholars "submitting documents to archives for retrieval by anonymous FTP in order to broaden the prepublication peer review process" (Silberger 1995, p. 105). Tomer (1992) speculates that when and if Congress finally enacts legislation creating the National Digital Library, full-text libraries will be converted into machine-readable format and then made available for FTP. The nearly 25 terabytes of data that make up the holdings of the Library of Congress would form the backbone of the electronic library. Project Gutenberg at the College of St. Benedict is another attempt to provide access to public domain books via FTP (Tomer 1992).

Many continue to hold the view that academic applications of network resources are chiefly the province of computer engineers and physical scientists.

> *If, however, libraries have been and continue to be the laboratories for research in the humanities (and to a lesser degree, in the social sciences), then the availability of library catalogs and other library resources over the Internet (and other wide-area networks) may be as much, if not more of, a boon for the linguist as for the physicist . . .* (Tomer 1992, p. 90).

Tomer's aside notwithstanding, social science research stands to benefit significantly from new information technologies. If they were merely to assist researchers perform the same tasks more efficiently and effectively, Miller (1995) observes, then the new technologies would be valuable indeed. However, the scope and content of social science research are also directly affected. Other scholarly disciplines, such as art, anthropology, history, and economics, are also being revolutionized by information technologies. The transforming potential of powerful data retrieval mechanisms have not only begun to alter the methods of research but to redefine, in the process, the very meaning of research.

The new technologies also enable scholars to communicate and collaborate with others around the world. Silberger (1995) quotes Harnad who has coined the expression *scholarly skywriting* to denote how computer-mediated communication, particularly international e-mail, has fostered growth in scholarly discussion groups. Online scholarly discussion groups "can easily encompass the informality of a casual dialogue, the pseudo-formality of conference presentations, the social mechanisms of the invisible college, and, increasingly, the rigor of scholarly publication" (Muns 1995, p. 152). Two of the distribution mechanisms are Usenet newsgroups and the Internet listservers. Both are online discussion groups differing mainly in the degree of control a scholar exercises regarding the content and volume of e-mail solicited. So much scholarly collaboration has resulted, often transcending traditional disciplinary boundaries, that Yavarkovsky (1990) has aptly nicknamed the network "the collaboratory."

Network collaboration also makes possible the creation of original modes of research. In the social sciences, for instance, network collaboration may lead to the development of powerful new analytic instruments. The same case might be made for other disciplines, particularly in the humanities, where new, discipline-specific, analytic research tools are even less likely to be developed without the kinds of collaborative efforts made possible by network affiliation.

Obviously not all faculty, no matter their discipline, elect to become network literate, though Muns (1995) contends using the network requires no more time or intellect than learning to play ordinary card or board games. In such instances, another kind of compromise makes perfect sense.

> *Researchers are seeking out and forming collaborative teams with support personnel on their campus, particularly librarians and computer center personnel. Although the networks offer powerful possibilities, they require specialized knowledge of hardware, software, telecommunications, and information retrieval and manipulation techniques. It simply is impractical for someone with specialized knowledge in one area to spend the time to master these other specialties* (Silberger 1995, p. 106).

By extension, the scholarships of integration and application are served by accelerated online communication and collaboration. The Internet has made possible a collapse of the historic barriers between faculty and other departments, corporations, and federal and state government agencies. The WWW alone contains thousands of Web sites designed to help faculty identify and locate other researchers with interests and expertise similar to their own, regardless of formal or academic standing. Increasingly, institutions, corporations, and government agencies are establishing electronic versions of technology transfer offices, like the ones

at Stanford University (www.leland.standford.edu/group/
OTL/external.html) *(Accessed June 30, 1997)* or the vari-
ous U.S. laboratories, such as Argonne, Sandia, and Oak
Ridge (www.galaxy.einet.net/GJ/tech/transfer). *(Accessed
June 30, 1997).*

Today faculty have a range of options with respect to collaborative research. Should they choose to collaborate, faculty
may follow the traditional path of working locally with other
scholars and being assisted by students on projects of shared
interest. "Two sociologists working together on a study of the
attitudes of residents of a local subsidized housing project is
an example of this kind of traditional teamwork" (Austin and
Baldwin 1991, p. 20). Or faculty may opt to participate in
large-scale, crossdisciplinary research projects involving a
multifaceted research problem. "The Manhattan Project that
secretly employed large numbers of scientists in the research
that led to production of the first atomic bomb is perhaps the
best known example of modern teamwork" (Austin and
Baldwin 1991, p. 20). However, whether faculty choose to
engage in "traditional" or "modern" collaboration, new technologies offer scholars opportunities to develop and apply
original, discipline-specific, analytic tools of research; to cultivate new working relationships with scholars around the
globe; and to explore subjects of mutual scholarly interest
beyond disciplinary and institutional boundaries.

New Epistemologies for Different
Forms of Scholarship?

No discussion of the nature of scholarship would be complete, especially one proposing a reconceptualization, without confronting issues of epistemology, such as those addressing different kinds of knowledge and the degrees of
certainty for each kind. The prevailing institutional epistemology that underpins the scholarship of discovery is empiricism—what Schon (1995) calls "technical rationality"
(p. 29)—which posits that human knowledge derives from
what is presented to the mind by the senses or by introspec-
tive awareness through experience. Research of this kind
involves "rigorously controlled experimentation, statistical
analysis of observed correlations of variables, or disinter-
ested theoretical speculation" (Schon 1995, p. 29). Schoen
argues persuasively that if the new forms of scholarship
advanced by the Carnegie Foundation for the Advancement

of Teaching—the scholarships of integration, application, and teaching—are to mean anything, "the new scholars must produce knowledge that is testably valid, according to criteria of appropriate vigor, and their claims to knowledge must lend themselves to intellectual debate within academic (among other) communities of inquiry" (p. 27).

The proposed new forms of scholarship would most certainly come under sharp attack by traditionalists if the knowledge they produce is testably invalid by current empirical standards or, worse yet, if appropriately rigorous criteria cannot readily be established to measure its degree of certainty.

> *In such a context, a senior faculty member might argue that if you can't name the variables and measure their values, and if you can't create control groups or manage random assignment of subjects to treatment and control groups, then you can't possibly generate valid knowledge. In the absence of these conditions, he or she might argue, you're not doing rigorous research, it can't count as real scholarship, and it's not deserving of promotion or tenure* (Schon 1995, p. 34).

Two examples of the epistemological dilemma confronting the new scholarship, cited by Schon, recently occurred at MIT. In the first instance, a promising young junior faculty member in the department of civil engineering was denied tenure because the "research" he was conducting could not be evaluated by the committee on tenure and promotion examining his case. He had developed two complete programs, A and B, the first being an intelligent tutoring system designed to assist civil engineering students learn statics. Program B was conceived as a design tool that created a virtual environment for experimentally testing the structural load-bearing capacities of student-designed bridges and trusses. Interestingly, the brightest engineering students rejected (or playfully subverted) program A, finding it uninspiring. On the other hand, program B, which frequently displayed unanticipated effects of load on structure, so enthralled large numbers of students to the point of sending them back to the textbooks to reexamine theory. The faculty member, who obviously knew "how to design software and get it to work in the design laboratories, did not know how to make 'research' out of it—that is, to read into his inquiry a question that could be subjected to empirical research" (p. 33).

> *But, of course, for any problem of interest to teaching and learning, insofar as it arises and is studied in the actual contexts of practice, one cannot establish true control groups, create random assignments, eliminate potentially confounding phenomenon, or, in general, meet the standards of normal-science rigor. Hence, there can be no such thing as a "scholarship of teaching" unless we change the rules that govern what counts both as legitimate knowledge and as appropriately rigorous research into teaching and learning* (Schon 1995, p. 34).

In Schon's view, the faculty member might have used what he observed of student reaction to his programs as a springboard for original research. However, the research would of necessity be "action research," distinct from but equal to traditional research and requiring appropriate criteria as a basis for evaluation.

> *Perhaps there is an epistemology of practice that takes fuller account of the competence practitioners sometimes display in situations of uncertainty, complexity, uniqueness, and conflict. Perhaps there is a way of looking at problem-setting and intuitive artistry that presents these activities as describable and as susceptible to a kind of rigor that falls outside the boundaries of technical rationality* (p. 29).

Thus, the young faculty member might have engaged in a legitimate but different form of research if the organizational culture had supported efforts to develop new standards.

In a related instance at MIT, Schon recalls how Project Athena was initiated in 1982 to study the use of computers in undergraduate education. A series of case studies were undertaken in four departments and, after a period of time, it became obvious to several members of Athena's Executive Committee that such studies, including the case of the civil engineer denied tenure, raised more questions than investigators could possibly hope to answer. Furthermore, the project, whose mission was evolving, needed a commitment from the full executive committee for its continuation. But when the new proposal was submitted, it was rejected by the full committee, largely on the strength of a remark made by one of MIT's senior cognitive psychologists and an influential member of the administration: "We don't know anything about learning! Nobody does. And since we don't, it's ridiculous to talk about doing research on how the computer may help people learn science or engineering" (p. 33). The cognitive scientist's recommendation to discontinue Project Athena was perfectly consistent with the prevailing institutional epistemology.

For faculty members seeking to pursue new forms of scholarship, organizational transformation would have to permeate the institution.

> *People in a position to influence the institution's promotion and tenure processes would have to learn how the design of educational software can be seen as legitimate research—the scholarship of application, or teaching, or both. The institution also would also have to learn how to critique such research, to create for it a community of inquiry capable of fostering an understanding of the kind of rigor appropriate to it—perhaps even to help young faculty members learn how to do it* (Schon 1995, p. 33).

To advance the scholarship of teaching, application, and integration, institutions need, by necessity, to become what Senge (1990) contends successful corporations are already becoming—learning organizations "where people continually expand their capacity to create the results they truly desire, where new and expansive patterns of thinking are nurtured, where collective aspiration is set free, and where people are continually learning how to learn together" (quoted by Tapscott 1995, p. 202).

Summary
The impetus for today's spirited debate over the nature of research and the role of the scholar can be traced to a number of recent social, political, and economic trends, outlined in section one of this monograph. For over 350 years, the American scholar has assumed the mantle prescribed by a society seeking definition and direction. Colonial college faculty prepared students for the ministry in a largely theo-

cratic culture. Research and scholarship was an amateur undertaking, privately supported, and outside the pale of higher education. An era of post-Civil War pragmatism produced land grant institutions that nurtured an agricultural and mechanical revolution. Faculty were enjoined by society to perform a service function by training young apprentices in applied research and technology. At about the same time, universities across the nation were absorbing and institutionalizing important elements of the German university research model, particularly graduate education. Today's American higher education establishment is an aggregate of three functions—teaching, service, and research—which at various times in our nation's history colleges and universities were called upon to perform.

Critics of American higher education today contend that especially since the Second World War, faculty have placed greater emphasis on the research function, to the detriment of teaching and service at a time when our culture demands the preparation of workers for a competitive and volatile economy. A new educational paradigm is called for, but the academy has been dilatory in its response. Recently, however, voices from within the academy have proposed a reconceptualization of scholarship, one that expands the practice of present-day research to include integration, application, and teaching.

The new computer-based technologies, particularly the Internet and WWW, are becoming increasingly necessary tools in the reform of traditional scholarship. Revolutionary breakthoughs in scholarly communication are paving the way for improvements in curriculum development, prepublication peer review, and technology transfer.

New forms of scholarship may necessitate a new epistemology. The scholarships of integration, application, and teaching entail "action" research that may fall outside the boundaries of prevailing institutional epistemology. College and universities must become learning organizations that foster originality and innovation.

New forms of scholarship may necessitate a new epistemology. The scholarships of integration, application, and teaching entail "action" research that may fall outside the boundaries of prevailing institutional epistemology.

CREATING A CULTURE OF QUALITY

Technology is the most purely human of humanity's features, and it is the driving force of human society. The defining benchmarks of the epochs of human history are the dominant technologies: the stone age, the bronze age, the iron age, the industrial age.
Lewis Perelman (1992, p. 25)

Work and learning have become synonymous in today's information economy. To remain marketable, workers must continually upgrade their knowledge base and technical skills. Likewise, competitive organizations must become learning organizations, ones that encourage personal and team decision making and equip decision makers with the most complete information available (Argyris and Schon 1978; Fiol and Lyles 1985). Equipped with the latest information technologies, employees create solutions where the rubber meets the road. "There is no substantial competitive advantage today," argues Tapscott (1996), "other than organizational learning" (p. 202). The more progressive academic institutions have assimilated this principle of distributed empowerment in response to major societal trends including the rising tide of consumerism. A transformation of organizational structure and culture, for the purpose of improving the quality of academic programs and services while potentially reducing costs, is beginning to redefine today's college campus.

The Structure of Academic Institutions

The traditional organizational structure for business and industry is vertical in design. The familiar metaphor is the pyramid, with power and authority emanating from the apex and descending to the base. With historic ties to both the church and to the military, corporate bureaucracy contains layers of middle managers functioning, in part, as conduits between upper-layer decisionmakers and lower-level rank-and-file. Personal initiative, creativity, and innovation are relatively foreign concepts to most employees in the traditional corporate environment, except perhaps for perfunctory opportunities provided by a suggestion box" The traditional structure is often unresponsive to the wants and needs of customers because the employees in a position to provide satisfaction are not fully empowered to do so.

The traditional organizational structure of academic institutions borrows heavily from the church and the military but increasingly from modern corporate bureaucracies. It possesses an administrative hierarchy, a formal division of labor, and a clerical support apparatus. It is not unusual for job titles to reflect a corporate bias: chief executive officer, chief financial officer, executive director, director of labor relations, director of human resources, director of MIS, director of public affairs, director of facilities. While they share other attributes as well, the differences between academic and corporate structures are noteworthy.

A number of models have been advanced to describe the unique organizational structure of higher education (Baldridge 1971; Baldridge et al. 1978; Blau 1973; Bartkovich 1983; Hendrickson and Bartkovich 1986; and Millet 1962). Millet (1962) and McClure (1993) contend that colleges and universities are communities of scholars, "loosely organized groups of semi-autonomous faculty who retain authority over the teaching and research processes" (McClure 1993, p. 48). In a subsequent publication, however, Millet (1978) acknowledges that the collegial model has limitations and  does an injustice to the variety of higher education institutions (Hendrickson and Bartkovich 1986). Baldridge (1971) proposes a political model, one that pits three interest groups—faculty, students, and administrators—against one another in pursuit of organizational control. However, Baldridge's typology was produced at a time in which campus protest and confrontation were quite common. Finally, Blau (1973) presents a model, later supported by Baldridge et al. (1978) and further enhanced by Hendrickson and Bartkovich (1986), which addresses both institutional variables and political processes. In Blau's bifurcated model of higher education institutions, two decision-making spheres exist, the bureaucratic and the academic:

> *The bureaucratic sphere evolved from those housekeeping functions and support services for which it takes responsibility. A hierarchy of authority and decision making was set up, divisions of labor were well defined, and formalized procedures were developed. In some institutions today, whether because of a strong board or centralization of authority by a strong president, the bureaucratic sphere dominates.*
>
> *On the other hand, the academic sphere is charac-*

terized by minimal definition of divisions of labor and formalized procedures. Authority lies with faculty who in the ideal state as a community make decisions in academic matters. This sphere is like Millet's community of scholars. In those institutions where it dominates, faculty have a great deal of autonomy and departments are the base unit of decision making. This is in contrast to the bureaucratic sphere which is relegated to support services only (Hendrickson and Bartkovich 1986, p. 307–08).

Building on Blau's bifurcated system, Hendrickson and Bartkovich (1986) have conceptualized a taxonomy of colleges and universities that accommodate political processes and institutional variables. The four organizational types are *bureaucratic, bureaucratic/academic, academic/bureaucratic,* and *academic.*

In *bureaucratic* institutions, the bureaucratic sphere, particularly upper levels of administration, predominates over all other decision-making bodies and activities. Faculty and departmental autonomy is minimal and labor relations are adversarial. Academic decision making, established at the board level by formal policies and procedures, typically resides with the dean or vice-president of instruction. "Some community colleges and some public and private baccalaureate institutions fit into this category" (p. 308).

In *bureaucratic/academic* institutions, the bureaucratic sphere continues to dominate decision-making processes. While faculty and departments enjoy very little autonomy, an academic sphere does exist in the form of a faculty senate and college-wide standing committees. When deemed necessary, the bureaucratic sphere supersedes faculty decisions even in those narrowly defined areas where they exercise influence. "Public and private four year institutions typically characterize this group. Some state colleges which are part of a state system with a history of evolution from normal schools seem to fit as the best examples of this taxonomic type" (Hendrickson and Bartkovich 1986, p. 308).

In *academic/bureaucratic* institutions, the academic sphere participates more fully in institutional decision-making processes. While faculty and department autonomy exist to some extent, institutional policies and procedures are in place, monitored by college-wide curriculum committees, to guide decisions as they relate to program changes and course approval. Faculty research is expected and encouraged, but this function will vary by school and department. "The classic examples of this institutional type are regionally prominent universities and land-grant institutions under strong centralized state systems" (Hendrickson and Bartkovich 1986, p. 309).

Finally, in *academic* institutions, the academic sphere—often noteworthy because of its cast of nationally prominent academic luminaries—predominate over the bureaucratic sphere, which serves mainly to provide academic support services and housekeeping. Course and curricular decisions, as well as promotion and tenure, are vested with faculty within departments or schools. This type of institution is undoubtedly the inspiration for Millet's (1978) and McClure's (1993) "community of scholars" organizational type. "The best examples of institutions within this type are prestigious public and private universities and some private colleges" (Hendrickson and Bartkovich 1986, p. 309).

Reforming both spheres of the traditional academic structure requires an understanding of several emerging technological trends, which have the potential to link individuals, groups, and spheres, forming new and unique strategic alliances. It will also require sensitivity to the diversity of institutional types, political entities, and faculty needs. On the virtual campus, the availability and integration of information resources, "where essentially everyone is connected to everything from everywhere" (Crow and Rariden 1993, p. 467), have laid the groundwork for a transformation of organizational structure and culture.

Reforming the Bureaucratic Sphere

We must occasionally remind ourselves that such traditional business practices as standardized accounting procedures, marketing techniques, and strategic planning have been basic components of college and university administrations for only a short time. Chaffee and Sherr (1992) trace the evolution of these practices on American campuses:

> *The demand for financial accountability in the 1960s ushered in standard accounting measures and practices, with leadership from the National Center for Higher Education Management Systems. Pressures to maintain*

enrollment in the 1970s brought the concept of competition and marketing—previously considered uncouth at best—to the ivory tower. By the early 1980s, the continuing struggle to maintain both enrollments and finances led us to strategic planning, our first sustained initiatives to think seriously about our environment, the services we render, and the need to anticipate the future (p. 2).

Fortunately, none of the gloom and doom scenarios envisioned by early critics of administrative reform have materialized. Nonetheless, a good deal of skepticism remains, particularly in the academic sphere.

Recognizing that radical change in higher education management is necessary to avert the crises that colleges and universities face today, many institutions are looking once again to the business sector for solutions. To improve quality, to increase productivity, and to reduce costs, many are incorporating the principles of Total Quality Management (TQM), also known as Continuous Quality Improvement (CQI) or Kaizen (Assar 1993; Brigham 1993, 1994; Chaffee and Sherr 1992; Entin 1993; Ernst, Katz, and Sack 1995; Ewell 1993; Garvin 1988; Marchese 1993; Seymour 1992, 1993; and Sherr and Teeter 1991). As Marchese (1993) recalls, "a few campus pioneers began their TQM effort in the eighties; the big wave of interest kicked in during the 1991-92 academic year; by now, it's hard to find a campus without a knot of people trying to implement the thing" (p. 4). Coupled with new information resources deployed to facilitate the transformation, the bureaucratic sphere is being reengineered for the next century.

In axiomatic form, TQM (an expression coined by the Department of Defense in 1985) is "meeting or exceeding customer needs" (Seymour 1992, p. 13). It originated in the work of statistician W. A. Shewhart at Bell Laboratories in the 1920s (Garvin 1988). Shewhart developed a statistical quality control method designed to evaluate product quality during rather than after the assembly process, significantly improving both the quality of manufactured goods and the productivity of line workers while reducing final inspection costs. In the 1950s, TQM advocates such as Juran and Deming persuaded the Japanese to rebuild their war-ravaged industries from the ground up, using organizational prototypes founded upon quality management principles.

As Masland (1985) observes, American corporations, battling stiff international competition and recessionary pressures at the top of the 1980s, began to take notice of Japanese management techniques articulated in such best-selling works as Ouchi's *Theory Z* (1981), Pascale and Athos' *The Art of Japanese Management* (1981), and Deal and Kennedy's *Corporate Cultures* (1982). Having come full circle, TQM has found a resting place where the theory originated, in American manufacturing firms. Its subsequent adaptation and implementation in the American service sector has not gone unnoticed by management consultants to higher education institutions. In fact, since 1985 when Fox Valley Technical College incorporated a quality improvement program—followed four years later by Oregon State University, the first major research university to practice TQM—hundreds of other colleges and universities have begun to embrace the principles of Total Quality Management (Brigham 1994).

According to Chaffee and Sherr (1992),

> *TQM is a comprehensive philosophy of living and working in organizations, emphasizing the relentless pursuit of continuous improvement. It encompasses an extensive array of tools. Its essence can be simplified to three ideas: defining quality in terms of the needs of the people and groups that the organization serves . . . , improving an organization's work performance or "technical system" (process analysis and improvement . . .), and improving the administrative system (personnel and organization issues)* (p. 3).

Underpinning these three ideas is the management philosophy of W. Edwards Deming. Deming's widely quoted "Fourteen Points" for organizational leaders are less a method of operation than a set of principles on which to establish an organizational culture committed to continuous quality improvement. They include such directives as, "Drive out fear, so everyone may work effectively for the company," "Eliminate slogans, exhortations, and targets for the workforce asking for zero defects and new levels of productivity," and "Put everybody in the company to work to accomplish the transformation. The transformation is everybody's job" (Chaffee and Sherr 1992, p.4). As these principles are absorbed and applied, the organization's culture is defined. According to Owens (1987),

> *Organizational culture is the body of solutions to problems that has worked consistently for a group and that is therefore taught to new members as the correct way to perceive, think about, and feel in relation to those problems. Over time, organizational culture takes on meaning so deep that it defines assumptions, values, beliefs, norms, and even the perceptions of participants in the organization. Though culture tends to drop from the conscious thoughts of participants over time, it continues to powerfully create meaning for them in their work and becomes "the rules of the game"* (p. 197).

Since an organization is inextricably linked to its culture (Curry 1992), Chaffee and Sherr contend that for TQM to be successful at higher education institutions, it must inevitably permeate the higher education culture, from top to bottom. There are a number of models available for implementing TQM. Seymour (1993) identified three common approaches: (1) the cascade model, in which top management generates the impetus, with the expectation it will flow downward; (2) the infection model, in which attempts are made to diffuse the principles of TQM from various selected organizational sectors; and (3) the loose-tight model, in which organizational leaders, encouraged by upper management, promote the practice and the philosophy throughout the organization. However, Brigham (1994) contends that such "low key, less strategically oriented approaches risk generating insufficient momentum or attention" (p. 3). Chaffee and Sherr (1992) have proposed steps for developing a TQM program on college campuses that are sustainable.

The first step, defining quality, varies from one setting to another. A factory floor, a surgical suite, and an insurance office are three distinct settings, each with its own standard of quality. At a college or university, quality may be defined as meeting the educational needs of its constituents. Such institutions obviously serve students in the classroom. But they also serve "taxpayers, parents, alumni, donors, and grant agencies" (Chaffee and Sherr 1992, p. 21). While Seymour (1992) insists on the use of the term "customers," Chaffee and Sherr prefer the less commercial "beneficiaries" to describe students, taxpayers, etc. Determining what beneficiaries need may require little more than simply asking them. "Their need could be as simple as clarity, accuracy, or completeness. It could be as complex as defining what students will need to know later in their lives" (1992, p. 21).

For postsecondary education, according to Chaffee and Sherr, quality has three components: design, output, and process.

> *Quality in design relates to both the output (for example, an academic program that meets students' needs) and the process (for example, the curriculum, instructional approaches, faculty, equipment, scheduling, and other factors that make up the program). Quality output means achieving the desired result. If all pharmacy graduates pass their licensure examination, the program could be said to have quality output. Process quality means that all the steps within the organization's functioning from beginning to end work effectively toward the desired goal. For example students in a series of useful, synergistic, nonredundant courses that make them effective engineers are experiencing a quality process* (1992, p. 22).

Each institution must develop its own definition of quality based upon a consideration of design, process, and output. Because beneficiaries and their needs change, the definition, as well as the standards by which it is measured, is likely to change. Continuous modification and improvement are central to TQM.

The second step, improving an organization's work performance, requires the identification and elimination of the root causes of problems by implementing what is variously called in the literature of TQM "the PDCA cycle," "Plan-Do-Check-Act," or "the Shewhart cycle":

> *First,* plan. *Spend adequate effort to understand the nature and causes of a problem, collect data on it, and use the data to inform your definition of the problem, your understanding of its root causes, and your decision about potential solutions. Use the data to develop a theory for process improvement—if we do such and such, the process will improve in these ways for these*

reasons. Then, do—*try your solution in a limited way to be sure it works—and* check—*did the solution work as intended, or does it need revision? Collect data at this stage too to be sure that the new process is better than the old one. Finally,* act. *When you are satisfied with the results, implement your solution permanently in all areas where it is relevant* (Chaffee and Sherr 1992, p. 41).

Chaffee and Sherr insist that the focus should remain on the work process and not on individuals. Since work processes typically leap over artificial boundaries imposed by organizations, a team approach involving individuals with varied skills from various departments is often required to identify and eliminate root causes of problems.

The third step, improving the administrative system, begins by acknowledging that organizational problems almost always originate from poor administrative decisions. Systems and work processes are created by administrators who alone have the authority to change what does not work. Furthermore, matching the aptitudes and abilities of workers to meet the specific requirements of work remains the prerogative of management. Thus, improvement of an organization's work performance will of necessity turn on the quality of management decisions. Chaffee and Sherr argue further that the PCDA cycle cannot be institutionalized without a supportive organizational climate and effective organizational leadership.

Organizational climate refers to "the atmosphere or style of life" within an organization (Masland 1985, p. 159). Similar to organizational culture, which describes "the shared values, beliefs, and ideologies" unique to an organization, climate attends more to agents that foster psychological well being of workers An organizational climate should place a high value on teamwork and cooperation. By eliminating the stress associated with individual competitiveness, administration creates an atmosphere encouraging team-driven solutions to organizational problems. Entrusting personnel with the opportunity and the authority to make changes as necessary "gives them a personal stake in the outcome, increasing their motivation to solve a problem involving quality and allowing them to enjoy the fruits of their work" (Chaffee and Sherr 1992, p. 64-65).

Altering an organization's climate requires leadership from senior administrative officials. Beyond fostering teamwork and cooperation and entrusting personnel to make changes in the work process, Chaffee and Sherr (1992) argue that organizational leaders need to develop a quality mission statement that serves to galvanize all employees in the organization.

> *Ideally, the organizational mission statement is also the quality mission statement. . . . Perhaps the most important feature of a good quality mission statement is its meaning to the people in the organization. There is no "correct" format or content, but it should address several questions: What do we do? For whom do we do it? Why do we do it? How do we do it?* (p. 71).

While Chaffee and Sherr (1992) go on to describe a number of tools to help employees work more effectively and leaders make strategic decisions, the essence of TQM is not to be found in technical tools or administrative concepts. Rather, it is a comprehensive philosophy that underpins the organization committed to continuous improvement. As such, TQM can be adapted not only to industrial organizations where it was first developed but to service and nonprofit organizations and to higher education institutions as well.

The Role of Information Resource Management
At a time when federal and state funding sources are flat or decreasing, reforming the bureaucratic sphere is essential in order to reallocate a greater proportion of existing resources to academic programs. If TQM is the underlying philosophy of a reengineered bureaucracy, then Information Resource Management (IRM) is the facilitator of broader information access. Only with such access by authorized users can the beneficiaries of higher education be fully served.

The quality of services delivered to undergraduate and graduate students is a function of IRM. Services such as admissions processing, registration, student billing, financial aid, and loan processing are ones often reported by students as unsatisfactory (Karns 1993; Kesner 1995). Just a few years ago, information resources were concentrated in a "Ptolemaic" infrastructure, that is a mainframe computer, or minicomputers, which processed registration, financial aid, transcripts, and other services. "At that point in time users were satisfied to take what was available in whatever form it was offered" (Crow and Rariden 1993, p. 469). On the virtual campus, however, "a more 'Copernican' view is forming, that is, the user has become the center of the resource universe. In this universe there is a vast arsenal of power and function" (Crow and Rariden 1993, p. 469).

For authorized users, virtually all of the institution's information resources are available almost anywhere—on or off campus—a microcomputer and a modem are available.

Powerful software tools are available that can essentially eliminate the technical expertise necessary to process either university-wide data or off-campus research databases. Intricate database management systems (DBMS) will allow local distribution of internal and external accumulated information. Students, faculty, and administrators will be able to ask and answer their own data-related questions from their desks without the assistance or intervention of a computer center's staff. Like the library, the computer center may thus also figuratively 'disappear' (Crow and Rariden 1993, p. 467).

If TQM is the underlying philosophy of a re-engineered bureaucracy, then Information Resource Management (IRM) is the facilitator of broader information access.

As Tapscott and Caston (1993) point out, virtually no institution— entrepreneurial or educational—has achieved a "comprehensive implementation" of the new IRM model (p. 11). Since no "how to" book at present exists, institutions are developing implementation strategies on the fly. For example, at Babson College, one of the best business specialty schools in the United States, a major reengineering project has been undertaken to reduce expenses by streamlining administrative services (Kesner 1995). The results of a four-year survey of primary beneficiaries (students, parents, employers) clearly indicated that while educational programs were "highly regarded," administrative support services were viewed as inconsistent and unsatisfactory (p. 94). A major premise of the reengineering design process was that a new set of information tools was required to improve access to data which were at the time "in a wide variety of inconsistent and largely inaccessible formats" (p. 103). In the estimation of the reengineering design team, appointed by President William F. Glavin, a radically different I/T infrastructure was necessary.

> To address this situation, Babson must develop a single, integrated information database that (1) captures all relevant customer data once, (2) allows for and indeed prompts the information owner to update and/or validate his/her records, (3) provides easy access to authorized users, (4) affords the capability to ask questions, develop scenarios, and conduct trend analysis from the data easily and quickly, (5) affords multiple views of the data in its most current and accurate form, and (6) provides access any time and from both on- and off-campus locations (Kesner 1995, p. 103).

An integrated database would permit the creation of a virtual (i.e., electronic) folder for each student. The virtual folder, interactive by design, would permit multiple and overlapping views of each and every student. Authorized users could access, for example, a democratic data view, initially created by the student "with system-driven reminders to keep the record current" (p. 103-104). Other accessible information views would be academic views, financial views, cocurricular views, campus residential views, external relations views, medical views, and other views as needed.

Creating access to such information, even to authorized users, contradicts significant historical and cultural precedents. To date, administrative structures and systems have generated "a never-ending cycle of audits, proceduralization, forms generation, signature authorization, and centralization of decision making," and by so doing, Ernst, Katz, and Sack (1995) maintain, "we have lost sight of our constituents and have created administration for its own sake and a culture averse to risk" (p. 11). Transforming an organization from one of mistrust to one that depends increasingly on employee judgment requires a philosophical commitment to employee empowerment, or what Chaffee and Sherr (1992) term "entrusting" (p. 65). Certainly the demand for transactional accuracy cannot be dismissed so glibly, but to achieve streamlined operations and to provide timely and effective service to students, Babson College has made the philosophical commitment to TQM and has entrusted employees to perform according to their capabilities and levels of authorization. Increased delegation of authority thus becomes a function of continual quality improvement.

Babson College's new electronic information network connects all campus buildings by optical fiber. Standard 486 personal computers, running Windows95 and employing point-and-click graphical user interface, will provide authorized users anywhere on campus immediate and uniform access to timely information. During a time of transition, a variety of servers will run both older, legacy applications and new client-server-based applications. Since the network architecture meets open industry standards, Babson College has positioned itself to adapt quickly as the technical environment matures.

Like many institutions, Babson College has invested in information technology out of financial exigency. With capital and library requirements underfunded by 50 percent and an additional 1.5 million dollars needed to fund new educational programs, the required revenues must come from some source other than increased tuition and fees, which are pegged at the consumer price index. Thus, cost savings generated by reengineering student administrative support services are seen as a source of considerable revenue reallocation.

As the experience at Babson College illustrates, Information Resource Management must integrate itself with Total Quality Management if institutions are to succeed in improving administrative services while simultaneously reducing costs. Ultimately, both TQM and IRM will have impact on the academic sphere as well, but as Coates's case study of Oregon State University's conversion to TQM in 1989 suggests, institutions must engage in pilot studies and "begin implementing TQM on the service side rather than on the academic side" (quoted in Sloan 1994, p. 458). In this manner, the PCDA cycle can be fine- tuned in areas that do not place at risk the central mission of the institution.

Reforming the Academic Sphere
Higher education enjoys a unique organizational structure. In the bifurcated model, two decision-making spheres exist, the bureaucratic and the academic. Any success TQM strategies might achieve in the bureaucratic sphere does not of necessity ensure success in the academic sphere. As Ewell (1993) recalls hearing during conversations with faculty, TQM is "all right when applied to the administrative side of the house but it's inappropriate for instruction" (p. 38). The

institutionalization of an innovation such as TQM will depend upon the degree to which it is valued by the particular culture within the organization. "Unless an innovation becomes valued, it will lack a constituency capable of lobbying for its continuation and ensuring that it becomes long lasting" (Curry 1992, pp. 11-12). In the academic sphere, TQM must be shown to faculty to be compatible with the norms, values, and goals of faculty.

In principle, faculty embrace the notion of quality in the work they perform. Most in fact are idealistic, discovering inherent rewards in intellectual pursuits, despite increasing economic and political pressures associated with the promotion and tenure process. Academic TQM, however, is likely to face stiff resistance from faculty for at least three reasons.

First, many faculty resist the notion—even resent the implication—that what works for business works for education. The language and aims of business, some contend, are inimical to faculty values (American Association for Higher Education 1994). For example, within the academic sphere, the idea of profitability is foreign, perhaps even repugnant. Curry (1992) articulates a concern felt by many faculty who have never had to address the economic concerns of higher education: "The word 'profitability' . . . might be taken to imply that higher orders of intellectual achievement are driven by profit motives and can be purchased rather than pursued by individuals driven by curiosity and the longing to learn for its own sake and provided by those similarly motivated" (p. 14). Or let us take the concept of "consumer" which Seymour (1992) insists is the preferred term for anyone benefiting from higher education. Ewell (1993) notes, "at few points does TQ conversation become so heated as around the word customer" (p. 42). Faculty are generally uncomfortable with the metaphor because the perception is that it considerably devalues their role, especially when externs "compare the acquisition of knowledge in a college classroom with purchasing chicken nuggets at a fast-food establishment, or even purchasing a car, unless one is attempting to illustrate absurdity" (Sloan 1994, p. 459). Though the application of TQM is more than the sum of its jargon, it is the very language itself that stands as an impediment to implementation.

Second, faculty are "independent entrepreneurs" (Chaffee and Sherr, 1992, p. 90), working within a loose confederation of schools and departments. On college campuses, teaching and research are individual, not collective processes. Where research is obligatory, faculty typically work independently, except on discrete projects with disciplinary partners. Teaching, too, is the province of the individual instructor. Faculty "own" the syllabus and curriculum. Furthermore, faculty members identify with their discipline as much or more than with their institutions, making it difficult to envision faculty participation in an organizational process designed to move the whole institution in a particular direction. Thus, critics would assert, "you cannot reengineer a process that you do not control" (McClure 1993, p. 48).

Last, many faculty are skeptical that "indicators" devised for academic TQM to measure the quality of teaching, learning, and scholarly activity will have even face validity and may trivialize the educational process and research endeavors. Before outcomes assessment came into vogue during the 1980s, agencies and institutions regularly measured quality by taking literal stock of "inputs": the number of faculty earning doctorates, the number of volumes in the library, the national test scores of applicants, and the size of the endowment (Chaffee and Sherr 1992). During the past decade pressure from external constituencies to demonstrate quality has focused attention on "outputs": educating students. However, progress has been very slow in developing adequate measures. "We are sure that just counting graduates is an inadequate measure of quality of instruction, but we have no other generally accepted measures" (McClure 1993, p. 48). Particularly galling to many academics is that academic TQM may invade the classroom or research lab with its insistence on process quality and with the widespread use of such tools as statistical process control to measure every classroom utterance. The level of cynicism concerning the statistical measurement of research productivity, for example, is reflected in a 1990 survey of the professorate by the Carnegie Foundation for the Advancement of Teaching. Nearly half of the respondents "were persuaded that their publications were merely counted, never read, even by those in the personnel process who insist on those same publications as a prerequisite for tenure or promotion" (Daly 1994, p. 47).

Despite these objections, many academic and administrative leaders are committed to exploring the potential of academic TQM. Chaffee and Sherr cite the instance of Ian Hau, who teaches business statistics to undergraduates at the University of Wisconsin. Using a quality team concept and the PDCA process cycle, Hau reports that during one semester student problems with overhead presentations, blackboard presentations, and computer presentations dropped, on average, more than 50 percent.

> *Hau defines the students as customers of the delivery of course materials, seeing them in other roles with respect to the course content and evaluation of students' performance. Hence, the quality team focused on delivery of course materials and defined students as the customers of the process. . . . Hau concludes, "'All changes were small, [but] data showed that the impact was large. None of [them are] difficult to understand. None of [them are] easy to do. It takes courage. The courage to identify defects. The courage to improve"* (Chaffee and Sherr 1992, p. 11–12).

Sherr and Teeter (1991), as well as Chaffee and Sherr (1992), review extended case studies of institutional experimentation with TQM in both the bureaucratic and academic sphere. In 1994, the American Association for Higher Education (AAHE) published 25 Snapshots of a Movement, profiling campuses implementing TQM. Responses to the survey instrument were quite predictably varied, as each institution identified such elements as primary reasons for embracing TQM, initial champions, key obstacles for TQM implementation (including faculty resistance), key successes and accomplishments, and predicted steps for further implementation.

Recent advances in assessment software offer at least a glimmer of hope that adequate quality indicators will be developed for the virtual campus. Virtual classrooms would seem to be more scrutable environments for objective, automated assessment than traditional physical classrooms.

> *The virtual classroom's electronic data storage, retrieval, and exchange system (i.e., the text of student and faculty transactions, communication logs, file structures, and information presentation algorithms that exist on the file server's hard disk drives) represent concentrated, structured, and highly accessible arti-*

facts of the learning transactions (Tucker 1995a, p. 49).

In terms of quality and assessment, the virtual classroom holds the additional advantage of being less obtrusive; that is, various kinds of measures can be made without the explicit awareness of participants. Faculty and students should be notified in advance of such assessment, but when it occurs, no special intrusive arrangements need be made. InterEd, Inc., has developed CyberQ, a software assessment approach to adaptive assessment and quality management (Tucker 1995a). Currently this proprietary software permits transaction profiling, syntax profiling, comment profiling, and predicate analysis. Albeit unsophisticated by future standards, CyberQ is a small but important step in the generation of higher education assessment techniques.

On a larger scale, the Western Governors University, a true virtual university, has built quality measures into its very structure.

On a larger scale, the Western Governors University, a true virtual university, has built quality measures into its very structure. The Western Governors Association (WGA) contracted with the National Center for Higher Education Management Systems and the Western Cooperative for Educational Telecommunications to design and develop competencies and assessment tools for local centers. WGA believes that shifting the focus away from "seat time" to the actual competence of students will help ensure the quality of its offerings.

Perhaps the most promising development for advocates of academic TQM is the practice in business and engineering schools of teaching it as an academic subject (Chaffee and Sherr 1992). The irony, lost neither on faculty nor students, is: how can an institution not practice what it preaches? According to Sloan (1994) this "inadvertent Trojan Horse" may finally "find a foothold at the core of academic culture" (p. 456). The curricular and pedagogical implications are at least intriguing.

Sloan is correct in his contention that while outside pressures have forced higher education to reexamine its values and assumptions, any transformation in organizational culture is likely to originate from within. Today, ethnic studies, gender studies, and leadership studies are generating theory and case analyses in areas of organizational structure, collaboration, and problem solving. As an example, Sloan cites the work of Nemorowicz and Rosi, who propose a higher education model based upon the needs of a global marketplace. Drawing on ideas "from feminism, cross-cultural theory, systems theory, and political theory, among other disciplines" (Sloan 1994, p. 461), their analysis of networked organizations resonates with the philosophy of TQM:

> *The traditional, pyramidal, bureaucratic structure is giving way to a networked model that relies on linked, autonomous units. . . . Networked organizations are characterized by consensual decision making, reduced positional inequalities, flexibility, commitment to a unifying purpose in the face of diversity, interactive leader-follower relationships and innovation. They generate more leadership roles and depend on self-governing teams of active participants. Networked organizations assume a more holistic approach to their members and expect that creativity and change will occur within the organization as result of interaction between leader and group member. . . . To respond successfully to the challenges of dynamic environments, leaders must understand and help build networked structures on all levels of social organization* (quoted by Sloan 1994, p. 462).

Inadvertently or not, many faculty are developing the concepts of Total Quality Management in a language that encourages dialogue between the two spheres. That such ideas are being generated and debated within and between the two organizational spheres "should blur distinctions that can be labeled as top down or bottom up, emphasizing the need to mesh or blend the roles assumed by faculty, management, and leadership when they collaborate in the process of change" (Curry 1992, p. 25). Out of this dialogue and debate will likely come a version of TQM appropriate to academic institutions.

Summary
Higher education institutions trace their traditional pyramidal structure to the church, the military, and modern corporate bureaucracies. While a number of models have been proposed to describe its unique properties, Blau's (1973) bifurcated model clearly illustrates the bureaucratic and academic decision-making spheres. Institutional variables and political processes influence the relationship between the spheres, and only rarely are the two in perfect balance.

Calls from external constituencies for academic institutions to demonstrate greater accountability and systematic improvement have sent many colleges and universities to the business sector for solutions. The principle of Total Quality Management, developed originally nearly 70 years ago by and for American industry, matured in the reorganized Japanese factories following the Second World War. In the 1980s, American interest in TQM revived under stiff competition from international manufacturers, particularly from the Japanese.

Less a set of specific tools than an underlying philosophy, TQM has been distilled by Chaffee and Sherr (1992) into three simple ideas: defining quality in terms of customer needs, bettering work performance, and improving administration. If TQM is the underlying philosophy, Information Resource Management is the facilitator of broad access to information. On the virtual campus, employee judgment replaces centralized decision making to resolve problems as they occur.

In the academic sphere, TQM faces stiff faculty resistance. Many see TQM as "another management fad from the evil empire of business" (Chaffee and Sherr 1992, p. 93). Others assert that TQM cannot work with faculty members who function independently, not collectively. Finally, some are skeptical that research, teaching, and service can be measured accurately by any of the tools TQM employs; worse yet, indicators of quality may trivialize the educational process. Despite these objections, TQM has made inroads in academic culture via classroom experimentation, inclusion in business and engineering curriculum, and in related theory in diverse disciplines. If academic TQM is to emerge as an agent of organizational reform, it is likely to come about more through faculty initiative than external pressure.

GOVERNANCE AND FINANCE CONSIDERATIONS

If you always do what you've always done, you'll always get what you've always got. Don Tapscott (1995, p. 208).

Bringing about the changes described in the foregoing sections requires that institutional leaders develop and articulate a vision of the role technology will play in higher education. There are cultural and political dimensions to such leadership. Culturally, the success of technology leadership is measured by the ability to influence organizational values and practices. "Leaders are expected to shape the culture . . . by creating new visions that organizational members can believe in and act upon" (Kearsley and Lynch 1992, p. 51). Politically, success is measured by the ability to counter the often conflicting aims of external constituencies and to affect public policies that may otherwise hamper educational uses of emerging technologies, such as telecommunications. In this latter context, "the education community will compete with many other stakeholders for influence" (U.S. Congress 1989, p. 150).

To a large extent, the governing structures of colleges and universities, particularly governing boards and trustees, determine what type of investment in educational technology is necessary and appropriate. "But in deciding what types of investments to make for the future," Hahn and Jackson (1995) maintain, "presidents and boards face a complex set of problems. They must decide what portion of their shrinking budgets should be allocated to this expanding domain. They must determine, from the array of technological choices, which options are appropriate for their campuses, distinguishing between the imperative and the luxurious, the essential and the grandiose" (p. 27). And, most importantly of all, they must contend with the "blooming, buzzing organized anarchy" (Waggaman 1991, p. 96) of the decision-making process in which progress toward a defined goal is rarely timely or linear. The subsections below address the following questions: (1) What regulatory issues need to be addressed by governing boards? (2) What guidelines are available for developing a telecommunications policy and implementing a strategic plan? and (3) What measures can be taken to contain costs?

The Regulatory Environment
As more and more colleges embrace distance learning, interactive television, computer-mediated communication, and

other melding technologies, a coherent strategy must be developed and adopted by governing boards to address the delivery of these alternative educational courses and programs. In today's education policy arena, a host of federal, regional, intra- and interstate regulatory issues require visionary institutional leadership in anticipating and shaping policy, not merely reacting to it.

The purpose of regulation is to satisfy the legitimate public concern for quality. But what happens when a college or university breaks from the traditional paradigm and delivers for-credit courses and degree programs away from their historic locale without establishing any physical facility or moving any of its faculty? Johnstone (1990) puts the issue of regulatory responsibility into focus by asking two additional questions: "Who is entitled to determine whether the public interest in quality is being served? Who will protect the public from less than qualified instructors and courses?" (p. 34).

Federal regulations

Because of the current volatility in the federal telecommunications policymaking environment, higher education faces both challenges and opportunities in forging a coherent plan for educational telecommunications. Quality, in part, becomes a function of the availability, cost, and type of services affected by government regulations on infrastructure and services (U.S. Congress 1989).

The changes in federal regulations as they affect the telecommunications industry are due in part to the shared policy-making authority of the Department of Commerce, the Federal Communications Commission (FCC), and the federal courts. Within the Department of Commerce, for instance, the National Telecommunication and Information Administration (NTIA) coordinates the policy-making agenda of the executive branch. The FCC, on the other hand, oversees broadcast, cable, and telephone industries. However, the telephone industries have been dramatically affected by federal court rulings such as the Modification of Final Judgment (MFJ), administered by U.S. District Court Judge Harold Greene, which broke up the Bell System into regional components, or Regional Bell Operating Companies (RBOCs). The MFJ prohibits the so-called Baby Bells from providing long distance services and restricts the information services they can provide. They presently provide the pipeline for content created by others. "The content restrictions were implemented to ensure that the owner of the public information highway, the RBOCs, would not also control what content was carried over that highway" (U.S. Congress 1989, p. 150).

As a direct consequence of shifting federal policies and regulations, the availability, cost, and types of services higher education can offer are today somewhat restricted. For example, availability of educational services has been directly influenced by federal policy. The FCC, which controls the licensing of satellites, also allocates microwave frequencies for the transmission of educational programming on the Instructional Television Fixed Service (ITFS). During the 1980s, the FCC eliminated underutilized spectrum from ITFS. Licensees of the remaining frequencies were subsequently permitted to lease channels to other users, thereby further restricting access to educational providers. In addition, the RBOCs continue to lobby Congress for some relaxation of regulations imposed by the MFJ in order to develop more advanced telecommunications services, particularly in response to corporate and education customers seeking greater videoconferencing capabilities (U.S. Congress 1989).

Costs remain an important issue for higher education providers since the FCC monitors and regulates long distance rates. In some jurisdictions, the FCC has established a set price for services rather than a guaranteed rate of return for carriers. "Some expect these changes to lead to lower costs for users, while others worry that locking in prices as technology gets cheaper will actually disadvantage users" (U.S. Congress, 1989, p. 151).

Finally, federal policies and regulations influence the kinds of services colleges and universities can offer. Currently, narrowband Integrated Services Digital Networks (ISDN) and advanced switching technologies give educational providers the capability of simultaneous voice, data, and limited video transmission from point to point. However, on the technological horizon is integrated broadband networks, with transmission via telephone or cable. This alternative technology carries with it the potential for full-motion video and possibly other creative applications. At issue in the regulatory debate is pricing and depreciation rates for what may well become competing technologies. "Faster depreciation could encourage the deployment of new networks at the expense of higher prices for existing services" (U.S. Congress 1989, p.151).

Outside the educational community many other stakeholders, some with competing interests, have joined the debate over federal telecommunications policy. For higher education to develop an effective voice in the debate, stronger organizational networking at all levels will be required. As Schlosser and Anderson (1994) make clear, "It is the job of the various management and administrative bodies at each of those levels to consider the issues and construct policies designed to facilitate effective solutions which must evolve in concert with political and economic policy-making agendas" (p. 31).

Regional accreditation

The new paradigm for teaching and learning poses a unique set of challenges for peer accreditation. For over 80 years the Commission on Institutions of Higher Education (CIHE) has successfully adapted to change within institutions (Crow 1994/95). However, distance learning and the new technologies raise the issue of whether 20th-century standards of evaluation are adequate to the needs, in some instances, of radically reengineered institutions.

College and university governing boards have the opportunity and the responsibility to stimulate discussion and to help establish common criteria for institutional evaluation. A major focus for such discussion would be, to what extent are new criteria needed to evaluate institutions experimenting with or fully immersed in alternative forms of educational delivery? On the one hand, Goldstein (1991) warns against abandoning traditional criteria: "We need to steer clear of the intellectual trap that leads us to believe that distance learning is so inherently different from what we have come to define as traditional instruction that either it demands entirely different rules—which we are then unwilling or unable to promulgate—or it cannot possibly meet the established standards and therefore it is not worth fixing. Although neither is the case, experience shows that this reaction is painfully common" (quoted in Crow 1994/95, p. 355). On the other hand, Crow insists that traditional standards and criteria should be articulated "with enough flexibility to assure that we do not squelch important innovation" (p. 355).

Over the next several months, as regional groups approach the task of developing quality standards by which to evaluate alternative delivery systems, a main concern will be to avoid restrictions that are shortsighted. Steven D. Crow, Deputy Director, North Central Association Commission on Institutions of Higher Education, proposes a preliminary list of 10 "good practices" to inform such discussion:

1. *The institution's distance delivery programs have a clearly defined purpose congruent with the institutional mission and purposes.*
2. *The institution admits to its distance delivery programs students who meet the institutional admission requirements but who also have the capability to succeed in the distance delivery environment.*
3. *The institution's financial documents (e.g., audits and budgets) show sufficient financial capacity and commitment to support the distance delivery programs. That support includes appropriate administration for the program as well as development programs for faculty and others providing support services.*
4. *The faculty provide appropriate oversight for all distance delivery of education, assuring both the rigor of the curriculum and the quality of instruction.*
5. *The institution provides access to the learning and support services necessary for the distant-learning student to succeed.*
6. *The institution evaluates its distance delivery programs on a regular and systematic basis and makes the changes necessary to improve their quality.*
7. *The institution assures that its distance delivery programs facilitate appropriate student-faculty and student-student interaction.*
8. *The program delivered through distance delivery has a coherence and comprehensiveness comparable to the program offered on the home campus.*
9. *The expected learning outcomes for courses and programs offered through distance delivery are the same as those used for comparable courses and programs on the home campus.*
10. *The institution's system of distance delivery includes appropriate back-up systems to compensate for short-run technological difficulties* (pp. 355–56).

College and university governing boards have the opportunity and the responsibility to stimulate discussion and to help establish common criteria for institutional evaluation.

The challenge to accreditors in the long run will be one of definition. Traditional notions of teaching, learning, faculty roles and responsibilities, scholarly activity, organizational culture, and the residential concept of education are undergoing rapid transformation. And governing boards will best serve the public trust by (1) supporting visionary presidents and chancellors who grapple on a daily basis with change, (2) becoming more purposeful about preparing themselves for increasingly more complex roles, and (3) maintaining a consistent focus upon quality in a turbulent political environment and against competing concepts involving a narrower vision.

State regulations

For institutions developing instructional telecommunications programs, one of the most vexing problems is negotiating the maze of state regulations (Olcott 1992). "In some states there are higher education coordinating boards, departments of education, or in some cases, separate state agencies that act as regulators of institutions in their particular state" (Johnstone 1990, p. 11). Compounding the problem are issues of interstate delivery of educational programs, including jurisdictional and accreditation concerns.

In 1983, the Project of Assessing Long Distance Learning via Telecommunications (ALLTEL), sponsored jointly by the Council on Postsecondary Accreditation and the State Higher Education Executive Officers, released a report addressing for the first time major administrative and management issues associated with the regulation of intra- and interstate delivery system (Chaloux 1985). Johnstone (1990) further cites the pioneering efforts of the National Technological University (NTU) headquartered in Fort Collins, Colorado, and Oklahoma State University, both of which successfully finessed their ways through a labyrinth of rules and regulations.

Two additional examples suggest that much remains to be done to transform archaic regulatory practices. In the first instance, California State University (CSU)–Chico was invited by Hewlett-Packard to deliver credit classes to corporate sites outside California (Johnstone 1990). CSU–Chico encountered no serious opposition, except from one state's higher education regulatory board, which insisted on reviewing the operation to determine whether or not it met state licensing requirements. CSU–Chico declined, arguing that "the corporate classes were merely an extension of the classroom in California and . . . that the university was accredited by the Western Association for Schools and Colleges" (p. 11). CSU–Chico continues to offer corporate classes in that state and at other sites outside California.

In the second instance, the Illinois State Board of Education rejected the "instructional format" of distance learning because "seat time" and "contact hours" were not identical to those of traditional classrooms. In a 1990 memo, the board stated:

It has been brought to our attention that some distance learning classes are presently only offering two or three periods a week with students assigned study/projects on the non-instructional days. Please be advised that this instructional format does not meet minimum recognition (in Illinois) standards (quoted in Johnstone 1990, p. 11).

The problem of applying the same standard to two distinct delivery modes is that both operate under different pedagogical assumptions. Reilly and Gulliver (1992) explain:

The distance learning experience, particularly when it involves the use of technology, cannot necessarily be evaluated by the standard measures applied to classroom education, such as seat time, amout of face-to-face contact with the instructor, and the immediate availability of massive library collections and extensive laboratory facilities. In fact, since measurement of these inputs has produced little empirical evidence of the effectiveness of conventional classroom learning, using them as the baseline to evaluate distance learning is problematic at best (p. 12).

Higher education institutions can play a critical role by creating new models to deal with antiquated practices (Johnstone 1990). Tucker (1995b) warns, "Soon there will be territorial disputes as distance learning providers exploit the global market. Federal and state laws and the requirements of regional accrediting bodies have not kept pace with technological innovation, and it is likely that one state's attempts to restrict virtual education through phones lines, the

Internet, or by satellite will be met by legal challenge" (p. 46). If governing boards fail to remain vigilant, the future of educational telecommunications will be shaped by forces possibly serving competing interests.

Strategic Planning for Technology

Institutional governing boards are advocates for as well as guardians of their institutions' long-term best interests (Kerr and Gade 1989). As the corporate entity for colleges and universities, a governing board establishes basic educational, operating, and personnel policies. A board errs when it defines its mission too narrowly, such as when it performs administrative rather than policy-making functions. Micromanaging day-to-day operations prevents the board from devoting its full attention to broader issues. At the other end, a board errs when it relinquishes its duties of policy making, in effect becoming a rubber stamp for short-sighted, ad hoc administrative decision making. Successful boards today draw upon the collective wisdom of their members to resolve issues that, in some instances, challenge the very existence of their institutions.

No issue on the current agenda of governing boards is more timely or more pressing than the establishment of a technological and telecommunications policy and a strategic plan for its implementation. Survey after survey indicate that both higher education institutions and private and public corporations have invested or will soon invest heavily in electronic infrastructure to support distance learning, computer-mediated communication, and virtual classrooms (Green 1996a; El-Khawas 1995; Tucker 1995b; Martin and Samels 1995). These very recent trends have led Martin and Samels (1995) to conclude: "colleges and universities that overlook or misread the potential of these technologies may find themselves losing students to other educational institutions but also to corporate competitors" (p. 27).

Trustees must without delay educate themselves concerning the role of telecommunications in the context of the institution's academic mission. Given the very challenging economic and technological environment of the 1990s, it is no wonder that a great deal of recent attention has been paid to the internal educational activities of board members (Floyd 1995). Chait, Holland, and Taylor (1991) identify mechanisms by which boards create learning opportunities, including "conference reports, local seminars, role-related discussion groups, rotating committee assignments, internal feedback mechanisms, and external feedback mechanisms" (Floyd 1995, p. 101). Through these educational opportunities, a board can be expected to develop formative agendas for technology planning sessions.

In developing a telecommunications policy and implementing a strategic plan, trustees and academic officers will discover few models or programs that have been proven "both educationally and financially successful," and thus a college or university embarking on such an ambitious project is "largely without refereed guidance" (Tucker 1995b, p. 44). Recent literature, however, has contributed a number of guidelines and recommendations for taking the first steps (Crow and Rariden 1993; Ernst, Katz, and Sack 1995; Flores 1995; Gunawardena 1990; Hahn and Jackson 1995; Martin and Samels 1995; Tucker 1995b; and Zastrocky 1995).

- *Infrastructure investment decisions require a global institutional perspective.*

The initial costs for basic infrastructure are substantial, so institutional planners must possess a vision of how to organize and structure the new technologies in ways that support diverse activities on campus. For cutting-edge institutions, the new infrastructure must support developments in teaching, learning, scholarly activity, student services, and administrative functions (Crow and Rariden 1993).

Flores (1995) contends that institutional survival may ultimately depend upon wise investment choices in three critical technologies:

Satellite Delivery. *Satellite delivery provides an excellent way to convey full-motion video, live and taped. Research and development promise broadcast-quality transmissions in the next few years. Investment choices: uplink facility, production studio, receive equipment, audiobridge, personnel.*
Video Teleconferencing. *Live two-way audio and video communication from one location to another allow for face-to-face meetings without the expense of travel. This is a relatively low-cost medium for the delivery and/or reception of courses among campuses.*

*Investment choices: two or more video-conferencing
systems, digital phone lines, personnel.*
Computers and Networking. *Institutionwide E-mail
systems are essential for administrative and academic
applications. Human-resources departments accept
applications, post job openings, and search for available specialists by E-mail as a matter of course. The
Internet creates new international communities of
learners and new relationships among board members,
administrators, faculty, and students at a very low cost.
Investment choices: computer hardware and software,
file servers, computer network, access to the Internet,
management information system personnel* (p. 31).

* *Identify the immediate and prospective users of the system.*

Students are and will remain the most important people on
the virtual campus. Everyone else at the institution, from
trustees to secretaries, "is there to facilitate and support student learning" (Boggs 1995–96). Therefore, before technology
choices are made, it is important to define the target market
and determine the needs of the learner. Martin and Samels
(1995) warn that institutions chart a dangerous course by trying to cover all bases: "The most successful distance-learning
programs carefully choose one or two niches based on institutional focus, regional employer needs, and other market characteristics" (p. 27-28). The authors cite as examples Western
Michigan University and New Mexico State, which emphasize,
respectively, business education and teacher training.

Among the other considerations are: Will courses be offered locally? nationally internationally? How will prospective students be informed of course offerings? Tucker
(1995b) notes that "Reaching distance learning students
through university catalogs and other methods employed in
on-ground education may be ineffective and certainly begs
the significance of the new medium" (p. 46).

Prospective students must also be able to conveniently
access institutional offerings in the technical forms or models available. For example, "Many institutions have found
that library or workplace access is not sufficient to support
computer-mediated distance learning models. Students must
have adequate computing facilities in their homes or on
laptops" (Tucker 1995b, p. 46).

- *Distinguish technological from nontechnological issues.*

Too often trustees and administrative decision-makers become enchanted by the novelty and innovativeness of a new technology and fail to consider its global impact. Technological issues are only one part of the current reform agenda. "To a certain extent, the medium is the institution, but in the early planning stages it is important to separate technical issues such as the nature of the pipeline (phone, fiber-optic, satellite, etc.) and bandwith (compressed video) from pedagogical and academic issues" (Tucker 1995, p. 46). Institutional planners must initially consider what kind of learning environment they wish to perpetuate or newly create. Is there, in fact, an explicit teaching/learning model in place? Is there an appropriate or ideal level of instructor/student and student/student interaction that must be met by any new technology?

Another nontechnological issue concerns the impact of change on organizational culture. Crow and Rariden (1993) maintain that introducing technology is far more complex than merely deploying it:

> *It involves a fundamental restructuring of the work flows, communication patterns, and historical precedents that give stability and structure to the people who work in that organization. This implies that one needs to recognize the cultural and historical values that are associated with [colleges and] universities in order to effectively manage any change process of this magnitude* (p. 466).

Of course, at some point in the planning process both technological and nontechnological processes will merge, but they must be understood first on their own terms.

- *Do not confuse technological effectiveness with efficiency.*

In the past, instructional technologies have been marketed as reducing costs by increasing efficiency. For example, some popular software tutorials, developed by instructional designers, were programmed to convey information and interact with students in a very mechanical but efficient manner, as in the case of some developmental English and mathematics programs. However, in other instances, as

Students are and will remain the most important people on the virtual campus. Therefore, before technology choices are made, it is important to define the target market and determine the needs of the learner.

Zastrocky (1995) reminds us, "colleges have tended to use the new technology to become more efficient in performing ineffective operations. Often we have only done the wrong things better and faster" (p. 59).

To sustain academic quality during a period of intense scrutiny and accountability, institutions will have to adjust the focus of technology from mechanical efficiency to human productivity and effectiveness (Ernst, Katz, and Sack 1995). "This requires recognizing that information technology does not necessarily save time or money," assert Hahn and Jackson (1995, p. 29). "It may enable us to do some things that we cannot do now, such as provide students with feedback on their work via electronic mail, or to do some things better and more easily than is now possible, such as attain access to library collections and conduct research." And as Gunawardena (1990) suggests further, it may "provide an institution with the capability of serving a much larger audience and one that is not easily accessible by any other means" (p. 34).

But all of this may not be very efficient, economical, or necessarily measurable. As an alternative to traditional classroom education, the new technologies promise only to meet the needs of institutional constituents.

- *Cultivate technology leadership and encourage innovating behaviors among faculty and staff.*

Institutionalizing change of the magnitude proposed by higher education reformers will obviously require leadership. However, leadership is not synonymous with management, particularly in professional organizations such as colleges and universities "where [individuals] can act as if [they] are self-employed yet regularly receive a paycheck. [They are seemingly] upside-down organization[s], where the workers sometimes manage their bosses" (Curry 1992, p. 21, quoting Mintzburg).

Trustees and academic administrators can attempt to gain compliance by coercion, but the history of technology in education clearly shows that "the manner in which technology is implemented is more important than any intrinsic characteristic of the technology" (Kearsley and Lynch 1992, p. 50). As with any major organizational change, the people who are most affected must believe in what they are doing or "the inertia generated by innovation for its own sake will quickly disappear" (p. 52).

Institutions must plan for technological innovation by developing organizational strategies such as cultivating technology leadership and encouraging innovating behaviors. Although trustees and academic administrators must possess and articulate a vision, "communications and decision-making in professional organizations must be two-directional or the culture emerging from the change will not be shared" (Curry 1992, p. 25). Faculty and staff must participate as technology leaders, dissolving a much as possible the traditional "top-down" change that is unlikely to lead to institutionalization. Toombs and Tierney (1991) propose identifying and encouraging *idea champions,* "individuals who not only develop an idea, but also have the desire and determination to see the idea through" (p. 74). Idea champions must be specifically skilled in conceiving solutions to technical, cultural, and political problems. These skills are essential in every sector of the organization where problems arise. Encouragement, possibly in the form of incentives, must be considered if the required culture-building and organizational support for change is to be continued.

- *Consider the accrual of benefits when calculating costs.*

Total investment costs of educational technology systems are substantial. However, even before attempting an estimate of initial funding requirements, as well as long-term financing to keep the system operational, a few fundamental cost-related policy issues require attention. Chief among these is the issue of benefits likely to accrue from institutional commitment to advanced communications technology.

Higher education's expectations of significant benefits from investment in new technology is reflected partly by the fact that "two thirds of all institutions reported that their budget for instructional technology had increased this year [1995]" (El-Khawas 1995, p. 9). The issue of ascertaining benefits is put succinctly by Markwood and Johnstone:

If the costs extend access to and enable the success of underserved student populations in ways that fulfill the mission, then the costs are warranted; if the costs fail to address the mission or if they buy more tools than are effectively being used by the students and faculty, then the costs obviously outweigh the benefits (quoted in Levine 1992, p. 77).

Beyond this core consideration, several authors have identified important issues that may be difficult to put precise dollar figures on but institutions must address in any complete cost/benefit analysis (Barr and Tagg 1995; Boggs 1995-96; Gunawardena 1990; Guskin 1994a; Hahn and Jackson 1995; Jacobs 1995; Levine 1992; Martin and Samels 1995; Tucker 1995b; U.S. Congress 1989). These issues may be categorized as follows: (1) Will a major institutional investment in new technological systems attract new students? help retain existing students? provide more convenient access for present and prospective students? (2) Will it support existing teaching/learning models? support existing instructor/student interactions? support a variety of models and levels of interaction? (3) Will it offer the potential for automated assessment of the learning processes? the learning environment? assessment comparisons between virtual and traditional learning? (4) Will it make possible an expansion of the curriculum into new cutting-edge areas? (5) Will it stimulate new and different forms of faculty research? enhance existing forms of faculty research? (6) Will it contribute to general economic conditions by attracting new industries? prepare better educated and highly trained knowledge workers? (7) Will it help reduce physical plant maintenance and repair requirements? offer a better economic return than brick and mortar investment?

Undoubtedly, there are other potential benefits to be considered and cost savings to be realized. As Hahn and Jackson (1995) note, careful deliberation should not beconfused with obfuscation. The risks—and the possible rewards—are indeed steep, butthey can be mitigated by judicious planning.

Cost Management Issues

No aspect of educational technology is more critical yet receives less attention in the literature than budget and finance considerations. There are at least three explanations for this. First, no two campus technology systems are likely to be configured in exactly the same way. Existing infrastructure, engineering requirements, the scope of the system, and other factors make even approximate cost comparisons to existing systems difficult. Second, technological innovations come to market so rapidly and so regularly that concerns over compatibility and obsolescence make budgetary projections problematic. Third, electronic systems components are in many cases decreasing in cost while at the same time delivering superior capacity. For these and other reasons, "there are no simple formulas to help estimate the cost of a technology system" (U.S. Congress 1989, p. 79, citing the National School Boards Association).

No aspect of educational technology is more critical yet receives less attention in the literature than budget and finance considerations.

Important cost management issues can be analyzed by creating an individual *taxonomy of technologies* based upon the nature and mission of the institution. For discussion purposes, we borrow from a host of available taxonomies. Tucker (1995), for example organizes communication technologies by emphasizing "the nature of the relationships between the instructor and student as well as the relationships among students" (p. 42). These categories are one-way video classrooms, two-way video classrooms, two-way audio classrooms, two-way audiographic classrooms, desktop groupware conferencing, desktop videoconferencing, asynchronous desktop conferencing, and asynchronous/CD-ROM hybrids. In *Linking for Learning* (U.S. Congress 1989), the Office of Technology Assessment suggests analyzing eight elements that affect overall costs: instructional design, scope of the system, existing infrastructure, partnerships, engineering requirements of the system, financial arrangements, programming, and training. Gross, Muscarella, and Pirkl (1994) divide delivery technologies into owned and leased. All of these typologies are very useful and need to be incorporated into the discussion. However, Flores's (1995) three-part typology of "leading technologies"—computers and networking, video teleconferencing, and satellite delivery—are especially useful as they represent major alternatives for each institutional provider.

Computers and networking

Colleges and universities may wish to venture into educational telecommunications by building on existing campus resources. An inventory of current staff, faculty, and student computer workstations as well as personnel who can be reallocated would be a fiscally prudent point of departure

(Martin and Samels 1995). In order to accurately project costs for basic infrastructure, state-of-the-art microcomputers and peripherals, as well as upgrades and replacements, a few factors must be considered:

1. *"Computers become obsolete six years after purchase and will be replaced at an average cost of $2,500"* (Jacobs 1995, p. 34). Computer systems are evolving so rapidly that to remain on the cutting edge, institutions will have have to phase out microcomputers on a staggered basis. Jacobs (1995) estimates that a midlife upgrade of $300 will probably extend the life of a microcomputer the full six years. "Typical upgrades have been increased memory, larger hard disks, replacement motherboards, added math co-processors, and added communications or network capabilities" (p. 35). The figure $2,500 is arrived at by observing that for more than a decade market pricing has stabilized because superior capacity and built-in peripherals have been offset by decreasing costs of electronic components.

2. *Cost projections should reflect arithmetical—possibly exponential—growth in demand for computing.* Many institutions anticipate steady enrollment growth during the next decade (NCES 1995). Communications and computing needs, however, may well spiral during the same period. There are many reasons for this. First, within the administrative sphere, reengineering efforts will require significant computing capacity for college business processes, including but not limited to admissions, student financial services, and academic records and registration (Kesner 1995). Second, within the academic sphere, reform of the research function is likely to create new and greater opportunities for on-line scholarly communication and collaboration (Silberger 1995). Third, demand for round-the-clock access to library resources will require substantial infrastructure development, particularly at research institutions (Tomer 1992). Finally, and most importantly, far greater computing capacity will be needed for expanded instructional applications, including tutorials, explorations, applications, and telecommunications (Means et al. 1993).

3. *The technology infrastructure may easily represent one-quarter to one-third of the total investment in microcomputers.* Supporting the traffic for network interaction in both academic and administrative spheres will require continuous and substantial investment. Computer technology, unrelated

to individual microcomputers, will include "mainframe, mini, and server computers, wide-area-networking hardware, terminals, and multimedia peripherals," not to mention "LCD panel displays, hard disks, tape backups, and switch boxes" (Jacobs 1995, p. 35). Also to be budgeted are costs of furniture, electricity, and additional software. For the period 1992-2000, for example, the Maricopa County Community College District has budgeted $1.6 million of a projected $7 million per annum computer technology spending plan to keep the computing infrastructure current (Jacobs 1995).

Video teleconferencing

An increasingly popular technologically enhanced learning environment is video teleconferencing, or videoconferencing. Videoconferencing permits high levels of audio and video communication and interaction between an instructor at an origination classroom site and students at one or more remote classrooms. Live interactive video was at one time the sole province of satellite dishes, but a number of technical breakthroughs, particularly in digital compression technology, permits relatively economical videoconferencing over the Public Switched Telephone Network (PSTN).

Video teleconferencing systems differ greatly in their physical configurations and in their capabilities. Shapiro, Roskos, and Cartwright (1995) distinguish between "electronic classrooms," which support presentations and lectures for groups of 35 to 200 students, and "teaching laboratories," which support high levels of interaction between faculty and 10 to 30 students. Another major difference among systems is the degree to which they link visually to one or more sites (Ostendorf 1991).

Common features of most videoconferencing rooms are the smart lectern teaching station, behind which the instructor teaches; electronic presentation systems; networked computers; and response systems, which allow students to answer questions simultaneously (Shapiro, Roskos, and Cartwright 1995). To illustrate costs associated with video teleconferencing, there is the example of Wayne County Community College (WCCC), which serves the metropolitan Detroit area and introduced live interactive technology during the 1996-97 academic year. An electronic classroom was constructed on each of two campuses, Eastern and Northwest, linking two academic centers in Detroit. During the early summer of 1996, two traditional classrooms were renovated and rewired in preparation for installation of new electronic media.

For a projected investment of $120,000, both electronic classrooms are identically equipped with state-of-the-art video, audio, and control system technology. Video equipment for each class includes four color cameras, each with wide-angle fixed lens or 60mm motorized zoom lens; four 27-inch color monitors/receivers; and one VHS VCR. Audio equipment includes two ceiling microphones and two audio loudspeakers. Smart lectern technology includes complete cabinetry, which houses a control system base unit, featuring an acoustical wave touch screen.

Contemplated, but not factored into the originial costs, are such options as a desktop document camera to replace the in-ceiling mounted camera, a nine-inch graphics monitor recessed in the instructor podium for viewing of the document camera; a dual cassette audio player to be used with the system; a second VCR for recording the entire session; a slide to video converter, which provides the ability to view 35mm slides over the system (controlled via the touch screen); and possibly an SVGA/Macintosh to NTSC converter, which provides the ability to view the computer over the system. Costs associated with these options range from under $1,000 for either the dual cassette audio player or the second VCR to just over $11,000 for all options considered.

The above costs and equipment are based upon vendor lists provided and do not reflect other necessary expenditures. Not included, for example, are physical room renovation and rewiring, student desks and chairs, and network enhancements to the existing transmission system. The five campuses of WCCC are currently served by T-1 compressed video capacity, permitting a fairly common data transmission speed (1.544 megabits per second) and quite acceptable for education applications of video teleconferencing. Network enhancements to the system are estimated at approximately $6,000.

Based upon the results of a needs assessment, additional electronic classrooms are likely to be installed during the next few years on all five campuses within the system.

Satellite delivery

The use of satellite technology to transmit educational programming across town or around the country is currently a very expensive option. Transponder time is limited and demand has escalated making costs grow astronomically. Recent technological developments in compression technology promise to increase capacity and reduce costs. However, for many distance education providers, satellite transmission is a very expensive alternative to other available technology systems.

A satellite is an orbiting, geosynchronous relay station thataccepts signals from a ground-based "uplink" facility and retransmits them to various receive sites, or "downlink" facilities. At the receive site, the dish is aimed at the satellite and tuned to the particular frequency of transmission, or "transponder."

Initial costs of a satellite delivery system will depend on whether complete facilities are built or leased. Colleges should expect to invest upwards of 1 million dollars for a complete uplink facility (U.S. Congress 1989), including studio facilities, descramblers for scrambled frequencies, as well as expensive encoding and decoding equipment for the new digitally compressed signals (Gross, Muscarella, and Pirkl 1994). Individual receive sites can cost upwards to $18,000, depending upon the voice, video, and data transmission requirements of the program (U.S. Congress 1989).

Ongoing costs will also depend on several factors. Interestingly, costs do not increase for distances served as they do with telephone systems. So long as the transmission is within the "footprint," or effective ground area the satellite can reach, the costs are relatively fixed. However, other ongoing costs can be substantial. For example, transponder leasing can vary between $5,000 and $170,000 per month, depending upon full or occasional use. Another factor to be considered would be the type of satellite. Only two distinct frequencies are available, Ku-band or C-band, each with its own advantages and contract fees. Institutions can expect to pay between $200 and $600 for hourly use of either band. Finally, ongoing personnel costs at both uplink and downlink facilities must be factored in, but estimates are difficult to provide, given program requirements, faculty contractual agreements, and staff availability.

Since initial and continuing costs of a satellite-based system are high, distance education providers will need to base investment decisions on institutional mission, long-term strategic planning, and faculty review. Normally, to be cost effective, large program enrollments are required, reducing interactivity. Since they are not asynchronous, there are only so many courses that can be offered at attractive times. Of the satellite delivery models, two in particular merit attention. One is TELETECHNET, the statewide partnership in Virginia between Old Dominion University (ODU) and the 23 colleges on the Virginia Community College System. ODU offers third- and fourth-year courses by satellite, allowing students to complete a wide variety of degree programs at community college sites across the state. Another is the use of satellites to deliver graduate engineering programs such as the statewide programs in Virginia, Florida, and Maryland, to name a few.

Summary

As large sums of money are contemplated and eventually allocated for educational technology development, college and university boards face a number of daunting tasks, including (1) closely monitoring regulatory legislation and actively participating in public policy debate, (2) establishing an institutional telecommunications policy and a strategic plan for its implementation, and (3) shepherding resources by defining genuine institutional needs and identifying appropriate technological solutions to fulfill them.

Educational telecommunications has generated a great deal of regulatory activity. Distance education providers must stay abreast of federal legislation that affects the availability, cost, and types of services that can be offered. Another board responsibility is to work with member institutions in developing common criteria for institutional evaluation within their respective regions. Finally, education providers must negotiate the maze of state regulationsthat often adversely affect the interstate delivery of educational programs.

In developing a telecommunications policy and implementing a strategic plan, trustees are encouraged to reflect on a number of recommendations presented in the recent literature, including consideration of how technology will impact on global campus activities, ascertaining immediate and prospective users of the system, separating technological and nontechnological issues, avoiding confusion between technological effectiveness and efficiency, and cultivating technology leadership throughout the organization, particularly among faculty and staff.

Cost management issues can be addressed by developing an institutional taxonomy of technologies, which essentially matches available technologies to existing resources within the framework of identified needs and institutional mission. Special consideration must be given to infrastructure requirements to support such technology systems as networked computing, videoconferencing, and satellite delivery systems. Initial as well as ongoing costs must be factored in as well.

CONCLUSIONS AND RECOMMENDATIONS

Our economy and technology do not direct us; they give us a very wide range of choice. The future of the nation and of our educational system is whatever the American people decide to make it, whether they are guided by habit, or wisdom, or fear, or caprice, or good will, or sheer desperation. More than ever before in our history, the task is not so much to guess where we will most likely be, but to decide where we would most like to be. Robert Bicker (1967).

The preceding sections have described some implications of the new technologies for five critical areas of higher education: teaching, learning, scholarly activity, organizational culture, and governance and finance. Recent survey reports suggest that colleges and universities are just now crossing the threshold between modest experimentation with and mainstream adoption of information technologies (El-Khawas 1995; Green 1996a). Closely associated with this technological diffusion are calls for major reforms of our institutions. Two assumptions that underpin these efforts are (1) that the primary rationale for reform is increased productivity within the system and (2) that the new technologies supply the tools to implement and institutionalize these reforms. On the basis of these assumptions and because of the serious repercussions reform efforts are already having on the academy, a number of conclusions and recommendations are warranted.

Conclusions
1. A paradigm shift can occur only in institutions committed to comprehensive reform.
A true paradigm shift in higher education refers to an array of reforms in teaching, learning, scholarly activity, organizational culture, governance and finance. The object of such a shift is to adapt the global structure to fill a perceived need, in this case, the diverse needs of new-century students. Such needs recently came into focus for many institutions following a number of pressures on resources as outlined in section one of this monograph.

For total restructuring to occur, innovation cannot be implemented piecemeal:

If innovations are isolated in segments and not permitted to touch other parts of the [organization], they are likely to never take hold, they are bound to fade into disuse, or they will produce a lower level of benefit than they potentially could (Kanter 1983, p. 299).

Many past efforts at restructuring have failed because they narrowly focused on one or two elements within the institution. The remaining elements forced the innovating elements to conform: "Innovations could not change the structure; the structure changed the innovation" (Blount 1995, p. 200).

For some institutions major restructuring may be unnecessary or undesirable. Judicious improvements in key institutional components, such as information resource management or selected applications of technology for classroom teaching, may be the limited but appropriate focus of reform. In the meantime, regardless of the nature and mission of the institution, the new technologies have not "radically transformed classrooms or the instructional activities of most faculty" (Green 1996b, p. 28) and any true technological revolution, or paradigm shift, is likely to occur slowly and incrementally.

2. Attempts to change the classroom focus from "the sage on the stage" to collaborative learning are likely to fail without a substantial commitment to professional development.

New instructional technologies present both the teacher and the learner with numerous options for interaction and subject-matter engagement. In the teaching paradigm, knowledge comes to the student through the instructor; decisions about the kind and extent of interaction as well as the role of technology in the classroom reside with the instructor. Even in the learning paradigm, insufficiently trained teachers can easily fail to exploit the potential of the new technologies and bring old metaphors and techniques from traditional classrooms into virtual space.

In any new technologically mediated environment—for example, interactive television or computer conferencing—teachers inadequately prepared or not fully committed to the new paradigm easily slip into comfortable clothing. In an intimidating new environment, it could be argued, students would benefit from a more familiar and traditional pedagogy. Such an argument begs the question.

Attempts to prevent confusion and initial disorientation disallows the cognitive dissonance that is essential if learners (both students and teacher) are to progress into a new relationship that is no longer centered on the instructor with students' eyes focused on the front of the class (Royars 1994, p. 100).

Consequently, without a substantial institutional commitment to ongoing professional development and technical support, "technological solutions will predictably deteriorate into superfluous pedagogical bandages and boondoggles" (Kearsley and Lynch 1992, p. 52).

3. Higher education will continue to be market driven, requiring redoubled efforts to define academic productivity.

All will agree on the importance of quality in higher educa-tion, and many will point to general areas of alleged weak-ness: unskilled graduates, poor teaching, arcane research, and high student loan default rates. At a time when tuition costs are outpacing inflation, public confidence in higher education has declined. A 1993 poll conducted by the Public Agenda Foundation reveals that a majority of the public surveyed believes higher education needs to be overhauled, though it is unable to "draw clear conclusions about the quality inside academic institutions or programs" (Nettles 1995, p. 297). This general feeling of dissatisfaction with the performance of public higher education institutions echoes in the halls of state legislatures and in corporate board rooms around the country.

Within the academy this connection between quality and productivity trouble many, particularly faculty "who view suspiciously the unwelcome overlap between the values of higher education and business—a distinction between the service and the profit sector" (Gaither, Nedwek, and Neal 1994, p. 13). Nonetheless, traditional evaluation by "input"— library holdings, faculty degrees, entrants' SAT scores—has been effectively replaced by "output" measures—some very concrete measures of return on investment. This is as it should be, but the issue of academic productivity is still far more complex than what it first appears to be, particularly to external constituencies. The key will be to strike a balance

Many past efforts at restructur- ing have failed because they narrowly focused on one or two elements within the institution.

between serving the state's economy through career preparation and asserting the values associated with a broad liberal education.

4. New constituencies appear to be well served by a variety of available distance learning venues.

Like the new technologies themselves, distance learning programs have moved beyond being marginal curiosities and have entered the mainstream of higher education. In just the past five years, the number of colleges and universities offering one or more distance learning venues has increased tenfold, from less than 3 percent at the top of the decade to more than 30 percent by middecade (Tucker 1995b).

The sudden interest in and explosive growth of distance learning can be directly attributed to a pent up demand by older working adults for whom various constraints prevent regular attendance on campus (Levine 1992). Time, distance, child care, transportation, and work and family responsibilities have forced urban, suburban, and rural workers to turn to institutions with innovative, technologically mediated programs (Hezel and Dirr 1991). Empirical research on the effectiveness of distance learning is sparse and usually based upon isolated cases and studies, and the costs associated with the more sophisticated venues are high. However, many colleges and universities see no alternative but to invest substantially in such programs, given the commitments of competing institutions and corporate entities that have positioned themselves to attract these new and growing constituencies.

5. The TQM movement has made impressive inroads in higher education administration; however, very little penetration has occurred where it most matters—on the academic side of the institution.

In just a few short years TQM implementation efforts have grown exponentially on campuses across the nation (Ewell 1993). Many institutions report startling successes—among office teams, faculty teams, and even student teams (American Association for Higher Education 1994). But is TQM really any different from earlier fads applied to the academic enterprise, like Management by Objectives and Zero-Based Budgeting? The claim is made by both theorists and practitioners that TQM "demands fundamental change in academic structures and in the way the actual work is done" (Ewell 1993, p. 38), which suggests a considerably different approach than the kinds of management impositions attempted previously. Where is TQM going? Brigham (1994) expects, "Success in the early stages of TQM will be measured by the number of team achievements, the simplification of important processes, and the reduction of costs" (p. 5). However, success using TQM in addressing higher education's most pressing concerns, teaching and learning, is far less certain.

TQM grew out of the technology of statistical process control and seeks to reduce variations in production or outcome. In an academic setting, this would essentially require, for example, the elimination of course grades because mastery learning objectives would hold. Students would master the subject or they would not. As Ewell (1993) correctly notes, this might work particularly well for developmental classes or ones in which the absorption of declarative knowledge could be easily or essentially measured. "But in the realm of higher-order thinking and the traditional domain of liberal education—where the development of individual voice and style becomes a paramount value—the answer is far from clear" (p. 42). Before TQM can be implemented in any meaningful way on the academic side of the institution, a number of fundamental issues relating to assessment, organizational culture, and institutional mission must be addressed.

Empirical research on the effectiveness of distance learning is sparse and usually based upon isolated cases and studies, and the costs associated with the more sophisticated venues are high.

6. Even as instructional use of technology rises, institutional support for applications development has been dilatory.

A very disturbing trend has emerged from six years of *Campus Computing* (1990–95) survey data: the small proportion of campuses supporting and rewarding faculty development of courseware has remained virtually unchanged (Geoghegan 1996). The implication for both teaching and the scholarship of teaching is quite serious.

As mainstream faculty more fully explore the instructional uses of computer simulations, scientific imagery, the Internet, and other applications, campuses do not appear well positioned to deal with a looming crisis in technology supply and demand. Imminent strains on infrastructure are likely to be exacerbated by the lack of quality software supporting curriculum reform and course design. Furthermore, the current tenure and reward system continues to discourage faculty from investing the time necessary to create instructional technology applications (DeLoughry 1993; Diamond 1994; Turner 1987). The National Project on Institutional Priorities and Faculty Rewards has performed an invaluable service by defining precisely how the development of instructional software could be considered a scholarly work. Software creation should be considered part of the faculty dossier if it "requires a high level of discipline-related experience; breaks new ground or is innovative; can be replicated or elaborated; can be documented; can be peer-reviewed; and has impact on . . . the discipline itself" (Cartwright 1994b, p. 27).

Unfortunately, until tenure and promotion committees can be made to understand and appreciate software development as part of a broader reconceptualization of scholarship, faculty will continue to concentrate on more traditional activities within their disciplines.

7. The historic commitment to core values in traditional undergraduate education has wavered; the same vacillation threatens to undermine general education requirements in electronically delivered certificate and degree programs.

A recent report from the National Association of Scholars, *The Dissolution of General Education: 1914–1993* (1996), confirms what most academics have witnessed for years: the undergraduate curriculum has lost its foundation of basic liberal arts course work, particularly after 1964, with a gradual "purging from the curriculum of many of the required basic survey courses that used to familiarize students with the historical, cultural, political and scientific foundations of their society" (quoted in "College Has Lost" 1996, p. 2). Within the context of technology and reform, it is difficult to see any strengthening of general education requirements in technologically mediated programs. Reverberating throughout the reform literature is a daunting lexicon, drawn mainly from the corporate and technological sectors: paradigm shift, reengineering, restructuring, total quality management, interface, the information superhighway, Online Public Access Catalogs (OPACs), and so forth. Used far less are words that reflect core values. Certainly, when the literature is reviewed, the core value of social functionalism—that is, the belief that higher education should prepare students for productive working lives—is implicit when not directly stated. The same can be said for the values of efficiency and productivity. These core values were conceived as the basis for educational reform in an industrial economy and continue today as the philosophical heart of today's corporate training programs.

No one would deny the importance of preparing students for an information/digital economy. To do otherwise would fail to serve the many new constituencies whose aspirations have been clearly articulated. As Simpson (1993) reminds us, "without the benefits of a broader exposure to liberal arts and experiences prior to vocational emphasis or professional specialization, such a policy has the long-run cost of denying students the intellectual breadth to cope with changing job requirements or broader roles without retraining" (p. 18).

A tremendous opportunity exists today for higher education institutions to distinguish themselves from the myriad proprietary colleges and for-profit corporate universities. Traditional colleges and universities occupy an honored position in our culture not just as important sources of new knowledge but as shapers of values, empowering students to improve the quality of their lives socially, morally, and economically. Now is certainly the time for the academy to reaffirm these core values even as, paradoxically, it reinvents itself for a world at once more complex and competitive.

Recommendations
Gilbert (1996) speaks of the inertia within our higher educational system, a system that measures change in years, perhaps decades, rather than months. Despite the rapid acceleration of computing power and the convergence of computing, communication, and content technologies, the pace of adoption among faculty and administrators, until very recently, has been slow. Thus, Gilbert believes it will be the next decade, instead of the next several months or years, that will prove critical. Still, in the absence of conclusive data with respect to wise technology choices and successful teaching/learning models, institutions must carefully prepare today for what is anticipated as a widespread integration of information technology into teaching, learning,

and research. Following are seven recommendations for beginning this process of integration.

1. Create a venue where key stakeholders can analyze major technology issues and purchases.

The Task Force on Technology in Higher Education, in its 1996 report to the American Federation of Teachers, cautions institutions that "new technologies are too expensive, too important and changing too rapidly—and the issues surrounding technology are too complex—to rely on ad hoc decision-making in this area" (p. 10). However, this is exactly what is happening at many institutions. Historically, policy-making and planning efforts affecting the entire institution are fashioned by upper-level management and governing boards. In today's fluid environment, such incomplete perspective fails to take into account the technological needs of faculty and students for teaching, learning, and research.

The American Association for Higher Education in Washington, D. C., has assisted more than 100 colleges and universities in establishing Teaching, Learning, and Technology Roundtables (TLTR) for the purpose of facilitating communication and shared decision making (Gilbert 1996; Task Force 1996). Technology leaders and other interested parties can browse the TLTR World Wide Web page at www.aahe.org/ *(Accessed June 30, 1997).*

2. Assert the value of technology-based learning from a variety of research perspectives.

Although there is a large body of literature on instructional technology and distance learning, most reviewers would agree that the research is mainly descriptive and theoretical, rather than empirical in nature. Most would also agree that more rigorous studies need to be undertaken to provide a scientific foundation for technology-based learning. Bork (1991) has proposed such an agenda for empirical research studies on technology-based learning. Moore and Thompson (1990), addressing the lack of sponsored research on distance education, recommends federal and private initiatives:

> *The implications . . . warrant investment of money, time, and human resources in a thorough, integrated national research program. This program should not*

only evaluate existing projects, but should institute . . .
rigorous research designed to measure the fundamen-
tal dynamics of learning and teaching by telecommu-
nications and its most effective organization, as well as
the procedures and policies regarding the development
of such education (p. 35).

Technology-based learning should be investigated from
additional perspectives as well, such as one proposed by
Boyer (1990) who contends that community college faculty
have a unique perspective on student learning, particularly
among students from less advantaged backgrounds. Possibly
working with coinvestigators more familiar with research
design and statistical analysis, classroom practitioners might
bring novel perspectives to classroom research. As Cross and
Angelo (1988) put it, "[t]he research most likely to improve
teaching and learning is that conducted by teachers on questions that they themselves have formulated in response to
problems or issues in their own teaching" (p. 2).

3. Establish quality standards for certificate and degree programs.

As instructional technology and distance learning enter the
mainstream of educational practice, increasing attention will
be paid to quality and assessment issues, particularly for programs heavily dependent upon telecommunications technology. Eleven Western states, having already taken the unprecedented step of endorsing the concept of a virtual university to
serve the entire region, are grappling with various criteria to
address quality concerns. Among the available frameworks
that may assist state higher education regulatory agencies,
regional accrediting associations and higher education institutions are the "Principles of Good Practice for Electronically
Offered Academic Degree and Certificate Programs" developed by the Western Cooperative for Educational
Telecommunications at WICHE (the Western Interstate
Commission for Higher Education) (Johnstone and Krauth
1996). These principles are offered not as a formal policy
statement but as a set of guidelines for institutions to follow
in regulating their own electronically delivered programs.
    National faculty unions have generally recommended a
"go slow" approach to developing electronically delivered
certificate and degree programs. More recently, the

American Federation of Teachers has gone on record as opposing "undergraduate degree programs taught entirely at a distance and views such programs as problematic at the graduate level also" (Task Force 1996, p. 14). The union contends that "teaching and learning in the shared human spaces of a campus are essential to the undergraduate experience and cannot be compromised too greatly without rendering the education unacceptable" (p. 14).

Individual institutions will indeed need to move cautiously with respect to electronically delivered programs, if only because they represent such a radical departure from the known terrain of educational delivery. Ventures in that direction must carry assurances that quality will be maintained.

4. Avoid pitting traditionalists against technology enthusiasts.

As data from the sixth annual Campus Computing survey indicate, instructional technology has entered the mainstream of faculty use at all types of higher education institutions (Green 1996a). Along with these marked gains comes increased pressure upon nonadopters to "go with the flow" and begin to employ technologies without so much as a rudimentary knowledge of their teaching and learning potential. The process of adoption thus becomes political—join the majority and retain status; remain a laggard and face ostracism. As simplistic as the process seems, it is fueled by the print culture's tendency to dichotomize practitioners into "good guys" and "bad guys" (Batson and Bass 1996; Gilbert 1996). Any number of publications have rather too neatly divided contemporary educational practice into "second wave vs. third wave," "industrial age vs. digital age," "learner-centered vs. teacher-centered," "atomistic vs. holistic," "Ptolemaic vs. Copernican," and so on.

The solution is to recognize the incremental nature of change and the power of curiosity and collegial encouragement. Gilbert (1996) reminds us that "no form of distance education or any other *widely applicable* educational use of information technology has yet proved so much more effective and/or expensive than 'traditional' forms of teaching and learning as to become a complete replacement for them" (p. 12). Technology leaders would do well to remember that for the foreseeable future a very wide range of classroom activities, from traditional lecture to virtual reality experiments, will continue to serve the needs of students seeking higher education.

5. Make collaboration *and* cooperation, *not* reengineering *and* restructuring, *the new institutional buzzwords.*

One quality criterion for teaching and learning with the new technologies is effective interaction—instructor/student and student/student. As members of a learning organization, faculty and administrators can take a lesson from the value we place on collaborate effort in the classroom. New network technologies should enhance existing channels of communication among faculty, staff, and administration and open up to faculty opportunities for collaboration previously restricted by departmental and disciplinary boundaries.

New emphases on interdisciplinary approaches to learning should stimulate collaborative faculty ventures such as team teaching and joint research projects by departmental colleagues. Administrators can play a key role in expanding collaborative options for faculty "by helping to create new avenues for collaboration outside normal structural (i.e., departmental) boundaries" (Austin and Baldwin 1991, p. 86). Although there are a number of problems that occasionally occur in collaborative arrangements, such faculty liaisons "can be especially helpful to junior faculty, women, minorities, and other professors whose careers could benefit from collaboration with colleagues" (p. 87).

6. Retain a strong commitment to adequate library staffing and funding.

Like the rest of the campus, the college or university library is sensitive to economic pressures and responsive to technological opportunities. As annual budgetary expenditures for the campus are reprioritized, library funding comes under increasing scrutiny. Since knowledge is becoming more distributed (remote patrons with computers and modems can "dial up" the library OPAC and conduct an on-line search of resources), a legitimate concern arises over short-sighted decisions being made to scale back on personnel, operating hours, and acquisitions. However, it is presently naive to assume that "virtual libraries," operated by a skeleton crew of database managers, will soon wholly replace existing facilities and services. First, "[a]lthough technology enables

The process of adoption thus becomes political—join the majority and retain status; remain a laggard and face ostracism. The solution is to recognize the incremental nature of change and the power of curiosity and collegial encouragement.

library technical services to reduce costs through networked resource sharing and automated processing, and by enabling libraries to offer new, user-friendly services, it creates increased demands on the reference department" (Silberger 1995, p. 104). For example, many reference departments are working to make other electronic information resources available via OPACs or on a CD-ROM network. Resources such as abstracts and periodical indexes, as well as a full range of electronic journals, monographs, and BITnet discussion group archives can be expected to come on line in the coming months and years. Second, reference librarians are especially helpful to scholars unfamiliar with international OPAC searching protocols in locating exotic resources overseas. Third, and perhaps most important, reference librarians continue to provide bibliographic instruction to undergraduates and graduates, individually or in groups, a service not to be underestimated as information resources become more complex and sophisticated. Therefore, when campus budgetary expenditures are reviewed, libraries should be accorded the same level of priority as other "new" communication and information technologies.

7. Prepare for success by creating the necessary support structures.

Early adopters of instructional technologies often experience what Alley and Repp (1996) calls "an instructional epiphany," a sudden realization that what had worked in the traditional classroom (the so-called "sage-on-the-stage" style of teaching) no longer worked in an electronic learning environment. As Alley explains, "[t]he traditional style of sequential lectures stumbled over the nonlinear communication, relational concept structures, and real-time interactivity that are encouraged by the new technologies" (p. 51). While Alley naturally bemoans the lack of "a team of seasoned experts" at his beck and call to solve instructional design problems (p. 52), Geoghegan (1996) contends that early adopters, such as Alley, actually benefit from jumping early onto the instructional technology bandwagon. Campus support structures are generally able to address the needs of the few who wish to explore and experiment with available campus technologies. A problem arises, however, when mainstream faculty attempt to make the jump in large numbers, as the most recent Campus Computing survey (Green

1996a) suggests is beginning to happen. Geoghegan (1996) warns that a crisis looms for institutions unprepared for widespread adoption of new technologies. Therefore, technical support for faculty must be as assiduously planned as financial or organizational considerations.

GLOSSARY OF TERMS

Asynchronous: Communicating on a delayed basis.

Bandwidth: The amount of information, measured in bits per second (bps), that can be transmitted through a network connection.

Browser: The software used to navigate the Web, such as Netscape Navigator or Microsoft Internet Explorer.

Client: A computer using the resources of another computer (server).

Cyberspace: The digital world of the Internet (coined by William Gibson in his novel, *Neuromancer*).

Download: The transfer of files from a remote computer over the Internet.

E-Mail: (Electronic mail) Messages sent electronically from one computer to another over the Internet.

FTP: (File Transfer Protocol) A computer program that allows the transfer of files from one computer to another over the Internet.

Gopher: An Internet-based repository of information in text-only format, not hypertext, that is accessed through a series of menus.

Homepage: The primary World Wide Web page for an individual or organization.

Host: A computer acting as a server.

HTML: (Hypertext Mark-up Language) The document format used by the World Wide Web.

Hypertext: A word or phrase on a Web page that is highlighted and linked to other Web sites.

Internet: A global network of computers that permits the exchange of information and data.

ISDN: (Integrated Services Digital Network) High-speed data communications lines with two channels, each capable of transmitting 64,000 bps.

Listserv: (Mailing list server) A program permitting individuals with common interests to exchange information via an electronic mailing list.

Modem: A device that allows two or more computers connected by a phone line to exchange information.

Navigate: To move from one Web site to another by clicking on hypertext with a mouse.

Network: A connection between two or more computers.

Newsgroup: A bulletin board system having a fairly narrow subject area as its focus.

Online: Being connected to a network.

Platform: A type of computer system with distinct capabilities, such as UNIX, MacIntosh, or MS/DOS.

Search Engine: Programs on the Internet such as Alta Vista, HotBot, Lycos, and others that permit users to search large databases for desired information.

Server: A powerful computer capable of handling multiple and simultaneous requests for information from clients.

Shareware: Relatively inexpensive software that can be downloaded from the Internet.

Surf: To explore cyberspace in a nonlinear way via hypertext links.

Synchronous: Simultaneous ("real time") communication.

URL: (Universal Resource Locator) An Internet address; for example, the Internet address of the White House is www.whitehouse.gov

Web Page/Web Site: A World Wide Web document containing text and possibly pictures, sound, and links to other Web sites.

World Wide Web: (WWW) A subset of the Internet that presents information in a hypertext environment.

REFERENCES

The Educational Resources Information Center (ERIC) Clearinghouse on Higher Education abstracts and indexes the current literature on higher education for inclusion in ERIC's database and announcement in ERIC's monthly bibliographic journal, *Resources in Education* (RIE). Most of these publications are available through the ERIC Document Reproduction Service (EDRS). For publications cited in this bibliography that are available from EDRS, ordering number and price code are included. Readers who wish to order a publication should write to the ERIC Document Reproduction Service, 7420 Fullerton Road, Suite 110, Springfield, Virginia 22153-2852. (Phone orders with VISA or MasterCard are taken at 800/443-ERIC or 703/440-1400.) When ordering, please specify the document (ED) number. Documents are available as noted in microfiche (MF) and paper copy (PC). If you have the price code ready when you call, EDRS can quote an exact price. The last page of the latest issue of *Resources in Education* also has the current cost, listed by code.

Adams, Cynthia Herbert, and David D. Palmer. 1993. "Economic Problems and the Future of Higher Education." *Academe* 78(7): 22–24.

Aiken, Robert, et al. 1995. "Report from a Committee of Hope." *Change* 27(2): 48–52.

Alley, Lee R., and Philip C. Repp. 1996. "Technology Precipitates Reflective Teaching: An Instructional Epiphany and the Evolution of a Red Square." *Change* (28) 2: 48–54, 56–57.

Altbach, Philip G. 1992. "Patterns in Higher Education Development: Toward the Year 2000." In *Emergent Issues in Education: Comparative Perspectives,* edited by Robert F. Arnove, Philip G. Altbach, and Gail P. Kelly. Albany: State Univ. of New York Press.

American Association for Higher Education. 1994. *25 Snapshots of a Movement: Profiles of Campuses Implementing CQI.* Washington, D.C.: Author.

Anadam, Kamala. 1994. "The Challenge of Institutionalizing Technology." Paper presented at the Annual Technology Conference of the League for Innovation in the Community College, November 13–16, Houston, Texas. ED 379 009. 14pp. MF–01; PC–01.

Argyris, Chris, and Donald Schon. 1978. *Organizational Learning*. Reading, Mass: Addison-Wesley.

Assar, Kathleen E. 1993. "Case Study Number Two: Phoenix." *Change* 25(3): 22–25.

Auld, Lawrence W.S., and Veronica S. Pantelidis. 1994. "Exploring Virtual Reality for Classroom Use: The Virtual Reality and Education Lab at East Carolina University." *TechTrends* 39(1): 29–31.

Austin, Ann E., and Roger G. Baldwin. 1991. *Faculty Collaboration: Enhancing the Quality of Scholarship and Teaching*. ASHE-ERIC Higher Education Report No. 7. Washington, D.C.: The George Washington University, School of Education and Human Development. ED 46 805. 138pp. MF–01; PC–06.

Baldridge, J. Victor. 1971. *Power and Conflict in the University*. New York: John Wiley.

Baldridge, J. Victor, et al. 1978. *Policy Making and Effective Leadership*. San Francisco: Jossey-Bass.

Banathy, B. 1968. *Instructional Systems*. Belmont, Calif.: Fearon.

Barker, Bruce O., Anthony G. Frisbie, and Kenneth R. Patrick. 1989. "Broadening the Definition of Distance Education in Light of New Telecommunications Technologies." *American Journal of Distance Education* 3(1): 20–29.

Barker, Donald I. 1994. "A Technological Revolution in Higher Education." *Journal of Educational Technology Systems* 23(2): 155–68.

Barnett, Ronald. 1992. "Linking Teaching and Research." *Journal of Higher Education* 63(6): 619–36.

Barr, Robert B., and John Tagg. 1995. "From Teaching to Learning: A New Paradigm for Undergraduate Education." *Change* 27(6): 13–25.

Bartkovich, J.P. 1983. *An Empirically Derived Taxonomy of Organizational Structure in Higher Education*. Unpublished doctoral dissertation. Charlottesville: University of Virginia.

Batson, Trent, and Randy Bass. 1996. "Primacy of Process: Teaching and Learning in the Computer Age." *Change* 28(2): 42–47.

Beaudoin, Michael. 1990. "The Instructor's Changing Role in Distance Education." *American Journal of Distance Education* 4(2): 21–30.

Berge, Zane, and Mauri P. Collins. 1995. "Introduction: Computer Mediated Communications and the Online Classroom in Distance learning." In *Computer Mediated Communication and the Online Classroom. Volume I: Overview and Perspectives*, edited by Zane L. Berge and Mauri P. Collins. Cresskill, N.J.:

Hampton Press.

Bicker, Robert. 1967. "After the Future, What?" In *Inventing Education for the Future,* edited by Werner Z. Hirsch. San Francisco: Chandler Publications.

Bleed, Ronald. 1993. "Community Colleges: Using Information Technologies to Harness the Winds of Change." In *Reengineering Teaching and Learning in Higher Education: Sheltered Groves, Camelot, Windmills, and Malls,* edited by Robert C. Heterick, Jr. Professional Paper Series, #10. Boulder, Colo.: CAUSE. ED 359 921. 57 pp. MF–01; PC–03.

Block, J.H. 1980. "Promoting Excellence Through Mastery Learning." *Theory into Practice* 19(1): 66–74.

Blount, H. Parker. 1995. "Restructuring Schools: What the Words Mean." *Contemporary Education* 66(4): 197–201.

Boggs, George R. 1995–96. "The Learning Paradigm." *Community College Journal* 66(3): 24–27.

Bonwell, Charles C., and James A. Eison. 1991. *Active Learning: Creating Excitement in the Classroom.* ASHE-ERIC Higher Education Report No. 1. Washington, D.C.: The George Washington University, School of Education and Human Development. ED 336 049. 121pp. MF–01; PC–05.

Bork, Alfred. 1991. "Is Technology-Based Learning Effective." *Contemporary Education* 63 (1): 6–14.

Bowen, Howard Rothman. 1980. *Adult Learning, Higher Education, and the Economics of Unused Capacity.* New York: College Entrance Examination Board.

Boyer, Ernest L. 1990. *Scholarship Reconsidered: Priorities of the Professoriate.* Princeton, N.J.: The Carnegie Foundation for the Advancement of Teaching. ED 326 149. 151pp. MF–01; PC not available EDRS.

Brigham, Steven E. 1993. "TQM Lessons We Can Learn from Industry." *Change* 25(3): 29–36.

———. 1994. "Introduction." In *25 Snapshots of a Movement: Profiles of Campuses Implementing CQI.* Washington, D.C.: American Association for Higher Education.

Brown, Judith. 1991. "Images for Insight: From the Research Lab to the Classroom." *Journal of Computing in Higher Education* 3(1): 104–23.

Carnevale, A. et al. 1990. *Training in America.* San Francisco: Jossey-Bass.

———. 1991. *America and the New Economy.* San Francisco: Jossey-Bass.

Carter, Deborah J., and Reginald Wilson. 1995. *Minorities in Higher*

Education: Thirteenth Annual Status Report. Washington, D.C.: American Council on Education.

Cartwright, G. Phillip. 1994. "Information Technology: Considerations for Tenure and Promotion." *Change* 26(5): 26–28

Cennamo, Katherine Sears, and Ginger Wellbaker Dawley. 1995. "Designing Interactive Video Materials for Adult Learners." *P & I* 34(1): 14–19.

Centra, John A. 1983. "Research Productivity and Teaching Effectiveness." *Research in Higher Education* 18(2): 379–89.

Chaffee, Ellen Earle, and Lawrence A. Sherr. 1992. *Quality: Transforming Postsecondary* Education. ASHE-ERIC Higher Education Report No. 3. Washington, D.C.: The George Washington University, School of Education and Human Development. ED 351 922. 145pp. MF–01; PC–06.

Chait, Richard P., Thomas P. Holland, and Barbara E. Taylor. 1991. *The Effective Board of Trustees.* New York: American Council on Education/Macmillan.

Chaloux, Bruce N. 1985. The Project on Assessing Long Distance Learning via Telecommunications. Project ALLTEL: A Summary Report. Washington, D.C.: Council on Postsecondary Accreditation. ED 271 102. 118pp. MF–01; PC–05.

Chickering, Arthur W., and Zelda F. Gamson. March 1987. "Seven Principles for Good Practice in Undergraduate Education." *AAHE Bulletin.* Washington, D.C.: American Association for Higher Education. ED 282 491. 6 pp. MF–01; PC–01.

Clark, R. E. 1983. "Reconsidering Research on Learning from Media." *Review of Educational Research* 53(4): 445–59.

Claxton, Charles S., and Patricia H. Murrell. 1987. *Learning Styles: Implications for Improving Educational Practices.* ASHE-ERIC Higher Education Report No. 4. Washington, D.C.: The George Washington University, Graduate School of Education and Human Development. ED 293 478. 116pp. MF–01; PC–05.

Coburn, P., et al. 1982. *Practical Guide to Computers in Education.* Reading, Mass.: Addison-Wesley.

"College Has Lost Its General Education Anchor, Study Shows." 1996. *On Campus* 15(8): 2.

Costin, Frank. January 1972. "Lecturing versus Other Methods of Teaching: A Review of Research." *British Journal of Educational Technology* 3: 4–30.

Cross, K. Patricia. 1981. *Adults as Learners.* San Francisco: Jossey-Bass.

Cross, K. Patricia, and Thomas A. Angelo. 1988. *Classroom Assessment Techniques: A Handbook for Faculty.* Ann Arbor:

Univ. of Michigan, National Center for Research to Improve Postsecondary Teaching and Learning. ED 317 097. 166pp. MF–01; PC–07.

Crow, Galen B., and Robert L. Rariden. 1993. "Advancing the Academic Information Infrastructure." *Journal of Research on Computing in Education* 25(4): 464–72.

Crow, Steven D. 1994/95. "Distance Learning: Challenges for Institutional Accreditation." *NCA Quarterly* 69(3): 354–58.

Cuban, Larry. 1986. *Teachers and Machines: The Classroom Use of Technology Since 1920*. New York: Teachers College Press.

————. 1989. "Neoprogressive Visions and Organizational Realities." *Harvard Educational Review* 59(2): 217–22.

Curry, Barbara K. 1992. *Instituting Enduring Innovations: Achieving Continuity of Change in Higher Education*. ASHE-ERIC Higher Education Report No. 7 Washington, D.C.: The George Washington University, School of Education and Human Development. ED 358 809. 90pp. MF–01; PC–04.

Daly, William T. 1994. "Teaching and Scholarship: Adapting American Education to Hard Times." *Journal of Higher Education* 65(1):45–46.

Darby, Jonathan. 1992. "The Future of Computers in Teaching and Learning." *Computers in Education* 19(1/2): 193–99.

Davis, Stan, and Jim Botkin. 1994. *The Monster Under the Bed*. New York: Simon & Schuster.

Deal, T.E., and A.A. Kennedy. 1982. *Corporate Cultures*. Reading, Mass.: Addison-Wesley.

Dede, Christopher. 1987. "Empowering Environments, Hypermedia and Microworlds." *The Computing Teacher* 14(3): 20–24.

————. 1990. "The Evolution of Distance Learning: Technology-Mediated Interactive Learning." *Journal of Research on Computing in Education* 22(3): 247–64.

DeLoughry, T.J. 3 March 1993. "Professors Report Progress in Gaining Recognition for Their Use of Technology." *Chronicle of Higher Education:* A19–A21

Diamond, Richard M. 11 May 1994. "The Tough Task of Reforming the Faculty-Reward System." *Chronicle of Higher Education:* B1–B3.

Dick, Walter, and L. Cary. 1979. *The Systematic Design of Instruction*. Glenview, Ill.: Scott, Foresman and Co.

————. 1985. *The Systematic Design of Instruction*. 2d ed. Glenview, Ill.: Scott, Foresman and Co.

Digranes, Jo Lynn Autry, and Swen H. Digranes. 1995. "Current and Proposed Uses of Technology for Training Part-Time Faculty."

Community College Journal of Research and Practice 19: 161–69.

Diulus, Frank P., and R. Bruce Baum. 1991. "Simulation, Creativity, and Learning." *Contemporary Education* 63(1): 35–37.

Doucette, Don. 1993. "Reengineering or Just Tinkering?" In *Reengineering Teaching and Learning in Higher Education: Sheltered Groves, Camelot, Windmills, and Malls,* edited by Robert C. Heterick, Jr. Professional Paper Series, #10. Boulder, Colo.: CAUSE. ED 359 921. 57 pp. MF–01; PC–03.

Dougherty, Kevin J. 1994. *The Contradictory College: The Conflicting Origins, Impacts, and Future of the Community College.* Albany: State Univ. of New York Press.

Dunn, R., J. Beaudry, and A. Klavas. 1989. "Survey of Research on Learning Styles." *Educational Leadership* 46(6): 50–58.

Eastmond, Dan, and Linda Ziegahn. 1995. "Instructional Design for the Online Classroom." In *Computer Mediated Communication and the Online Classroom. Volume I: Overview and Perspectives,* edited by Zane L. Berge and Mauri P. Collins. Cresskill, N.J.: Hampton Press.

El-Khawas, Elaine. 1995. *Campus Trends 1995: New Directions for Academic Programs.* Washington, D.C.: American Council on Education. ED 386 089. 67pp. MF–01; PC–03.

Ellsworth, Jill H. 1995. "Using Computer-Mediated Communication in Teaching University Courses." In *Computer Mediated Communication and the Online Classroom. Volume I: Overview and Perspectives,* edited by Zane L. Berg and Mauri P. Collins. Cresskill, N.J.: Hampton Press.

Entin, David H. 1993. "Case Study Number One: Boston." *Change* 25(3): 19–21.

Ernst, David J., Richard Katz, and John Sack. 1994. *Organizational and Technological Strategies for Higher Education in the Information Age."* Professional Paper Series, No. 13. Lansing, Mich.: CAUSE. ED 377 795. 25 pp. MF–01; PC–02.

Ewell, Peter T. 1993. "Total Quality and Academic Practice: The Idea We've Been Waiting For?" *Change* 25(3): 37–43.

Fiol, C.M. and M.A. Lyles. 1985. "Organizational Learning." *Academy of Management Review* 10(4): 3–13.

Flores, John G. 1995. "A Snapshot of Leading Technologies and Investment Choices." *Trusteeship* 3(2): 31.

Floyd, Carol Everly. 1995. "Governing Boards and Trustees." *Review of Higher Education* 19(2): 93–110.

Gagne, R.M. 1985. The Conditions of Learning and Theory of Instruction. 4th ed. New York: Holt, Rinehart, and Winston.

Gallini, Joan, and Nancy Helms. 1993. *Collaborative Science*

Learning in the Virtually Expanded Classroom. Paper presented at the annual meeting of the American Educational Research Association, April, Atlanta, Ga.

Gaither, Gerald, Brian P. Nedwek, and John E. Neal. 1994. *Measuring Up: The Promises and Pitfalls of Performance Indicators in Higher Education.* ASHE-ERIC Higher Education Report No. 5. Washington, D.C.: The George Washington University, School of Education and Human Development. ED 383 279. 159pp. MF–01; PC–07.

Garvin, David A. 1988. *Managing Quality: The Strategic and Competitive Edge.* New York: Free Press.

Geoghegan, William H. 1996. "In Response: Four Viewpoints." *Change* 28(2): 30.

Gilbert, Steven W. 1995. "Education Technology and Transformation." *Community College Journal* 66(2): 14–18.

———. 1996. "Making the Most of a Slow Revolution." *Change* 28(2): 10–23.

Goldstein, Michael B. 1991. Keynote Address. "Distance Learning and Accreditation." In *Distance Learning and Accreditation. Proceedings of a Professional Development Program,* edited by Marjorie Peace Lenn. Washington, D.C.: Council on Postsecondary Accreditation.

Graves, William H. 1994. "Toward a National Learning Infrastructure." *Educom Review* 29(2): 1–6. Available: http://www.educom.edu/web/pubs/review/reviewArticles

Green, Kenneth C. 1996a. *Campus Computing, 1995: National Survey of Desktop Computing in Higher Education.* Encino, Calif.: Campus Computing.

———. 1996b. "The Coming Ubiquity of Information Technology." *Change* 28(2): 24–28.

Green, Kenneth C., and Steven W. Gilbert. 1995. "Great Expectations: Content, Communications, Productivity and the Role of Information Technology in Higher Education." *Change* 27(2): 8–18.

Gross, Rich. 1995. "Defining the New Mandate for Distance Learning in the 21st Century." *Community College Journal* 66(2): 28–33.

Gross, Rich, Diane Muscarella, and Ray Pirkl. 1994. *New Connections: A College President's Guide to Distance Education.* Washington, D.C.: Instructional Telecommunications Council.

Gunawardena, Charlotte N. 1990. "Integrating Telecommunication Systems to Reach Distance Learners." *American Journal of Distance Education* 4(3): 30–39.

Guskin, Alan E. 1994a. "Reducing Student Costs and Enhancing Student Learning Part I. Restructuring the Administration." *Change* 26(4): 23–29.

———. 1994b. "Reducing Student Costs and Enhancing Student Learning. Part II. Restructuring the Role of Faculty." *Change* 26(5): 16–25.

Hahn, Robert, and Gregory Jackson. 1995. "The Keys to Wise Investments in Technology." *Trusteeship* 3(6): 27–29.

Hamilton, D. 1990. "Published by–and for–the Numbers." *Science* 250: 1331–32.

Harnad, Stevan. 1990. "Scholarly Skywriting and the Prepublication Continuum of Scientific Inquiry." *Psychological Science* 4(1): 342–43.

Hawkins, J. 1991. "Technology-Mediated Communication for Learning: Designs and Consequences." *Annals of the American Academy of Science* 514: 159–74.

Hayes, Elizabeth. 1990. "Adult Education: Context and Challenge for Distance Educators." *American Journal of Distance Education* 4(1): 25–38.

Haynes, K. J., and C. Dillon. 1992. "Distance Education: Learning Outcomes, Interactions, and Attitudes." *Journal of Education for Library and Information Science* 33(1): 34–45.

Heinich, Robert, Michael Molenda, and John D. Russell. 1989. *Instructional Media and the New Technologies.* New York: Macmillan.

Hendrickson, Robert M., and Jeffrey P. Bartovich. 1986. "Organizational Systematics: Toward a Classification Scheme for Postsecondary Institutions." *Review of Higher Education* 9(3): 303–24.

Heterick, Robert C., Jr. 1993. "Introduction: Reengineering Teaching and Learning." In *Reengineering Teaching and Learning in Higher Education: Sheltered Groves, Camelot, Windmills, and Malls,* edited by Robert C. Heterick, Jr. Professional Paper, #10. Boulder, Colo.: CAUSE. ED 359 921. 57 pp. MF–01; PC–03.

———. 1995. "The Dreaded 'P' Word." *Educom Review* 30(1): 1–3. Available:
http://www.educom.edu/web/pubs/review/reviewArticles

Hezel, Richard T., and Peter J. Dirr. 1991. "Barriers that Lead Students to Take Television-Based College Courses." *TechTrends* 36(1): 33–35.

Hillman, Daniel C., Deborah J. Willis, and Charlotte N. Gunawardena. 1994. "Learner-Interface Interaction in Distance Education: An Extension of Contemporary Models and Strategies for Practitioners." *American Journal of Distance Education* 8(2): 30–42.

Jacobs, Alan. 1995. "The Costs of Computer Technology." *Community College Journal* 66(2): 34–37.

Jauch, L. R. 1976. "Relationship of Research and Teaching: Implications for Faculty Evaluation." *Research in Higher Education* 5: 1–13.

Jensen, Robert E. 1993. "The Technology of the Future Is Already Here." *Academe* 79(4): 8–13.

Johnson, David W., Roger T. Johnson, and Karl A. Smith. 1991. *Cooperative Learning: Increasing College Faculty Instructional Productivity.* ASHE-ERIC Higher Education Report No. 4. Washington, D.C.: The George Washington University, School of Education and Human Development. ED343 465. 168pp. MF–01; PC–07.

Johnstone, Sally M. 1990. "Issues in Inter-State Delivery of Educational Programs Using Telecommunications Technologies." *American Journal of Distance Education* 4(3): 10–12.

Johnstone, Sally M., and Barbara Krauth. 1996. "The Virtual University: Principles of Good Practice." *Change* 28(2): 38–41.

Jonassen, David H. 1995. "Computers as Cognitive Tools: Learning *with* Technology, Not *from* Technology." *Journal of Computing in Higher Education* 6(2): 40–73.

Kalmbach, John A. 1994. "Just in Time for the 21st Century: Multimedia in the Classroom." *TechTrends* 39(6): 29–32.

Kanter, R.M. 1983. *The Change Masters: Innovation and Entrepreneurship in the American Corporation.* New York: Simon & Schuster.

Karns, Julie. 1993. "Redesigning Student Services." *Planning for Higher Education* 21(3): 27–33.

Katz, Richard N. 1993. "Silicon in the Grove: Computing, Teaching, and Learning in the American Research University." In *Reengineering Teaching and Learning in Higher Education: Sheltered Groves, Camelot, Windmills, and Malls,* edited by Robert C. Heterick, Jr. Professional Paper, #10. Boulder, Colo.: CAUSE. ED 359 921. 57 pp. MF–01; PC–03.

Kay, Alan C. 1988. Keynote presented at the EDUCOM '88 conference, October 25-28, Washington, D.C.

Kearsley, Greg, and William Lynch. 1992. "Educational Leadership in the Age of Technology: The New Skills." *Journal of Research on Computing in Education* 25(1): 50–60.

Keefe, J. 1987. *Learning Style: Theory and Practice.* Reston, Va.: National Association of Secondary School Principals.

Keig, Larry, and Michael D. Waggoner. 1994. *Collaborative Peer Review: The Role of Faculty in Improving College Teaching.* ASHE-ERIC Higher Education Report No. 2. Washington, D.C.: The George Washington University, School of Education and Human Development. ED 378 925. 100pp. MF–01; PC–04.

Keller, F.S. 1968. "Goodbye Teacher . . . " *Journal of Applied Behavior Analysis* 1: 79–89.

Kerr, Clark, and Marian L. Gade. 1989. *The Guardians: Boards of Trustees of American Colleges; What They Do and How Well They Do It.* Washington, D.C.: Association of Governing Boards of Universities and Colleges. ED 330 285. 236pp. MF–01; PC–07.

Kesner, Richard M. 1995. "Reengineering Babson College: Toward I/T Enabled Student Services." *Journal of Computing in Higher Education* 7(1): 94–107.

Knowles, M.S. 1984. *Androgogy in Action.* San Francisco: Jossey-Bass.

Krebs, Arlene. 1996. *The Distance Learning Funding Sourcebook.* 3d ed. Dubuque, Iowa: Kendall/Hunt.

Lambiotte, Judith G. et al. 1987. "Cooperative Learning and Test Taking: Transfer of Skills." *Contemporary Educational Psychology* 12: 52–61.

Land, Bruce, and Allison LoPerfido. 1993. "A Case for Scientific Visualization in Undergraduate and Graduate Classrooms." *Journal of Computing in Higher Education* 4(2): 3–11.

Levine, Toby. 1992. *Going the Distance.* Bethesda, Md.: Toby Levine Communications, Inc.

Lynch, Jean, and Catherine Bishop-Clark. 1994. "The Influence of Age in College Classrooms: Some New Evidence." *Community College Review* 22(3): 3–12.

Lynton, Ernest A. 1984. *The Missing Connection Between Business and the Universities.* New York: Macmillan.

Lynton, Ernest A., and Sandra E. Elman. 1987. *New Priorities for the Universities.* San Francisco: Jossey-Bass.

McClure, Polly Ann. 1993. "'Growing' Our Academic Productivity." In *Reengineering Teaching and Learning in Higher Education: Shletered Groves, Camelots, Windmills, and Malls,* edited by Robert C. Hetrick, Jr. Professional Paper #10. Boulder, Colo.: CAUSE. ED 359 921. 57pp. MF–01; PC–03.

Marchese, Ted. 1993. "TQM: A Time for Ideas." *Change* 25(3): 4–7.

Martin, James, and James E. Samels. 1995. "The Near and Far of Distance Learning." *Trusteeship* 3(2): 26–31.

Masland, Andrew. 1985. "Organizational Culture in the Study of Higher Education." *Review of Higher Education* 8(2): 157–68.

Massy, William F., Andrea K. Wilger, and Carol Colbeck. 1994. "Overcoming Hallowed Collegiality." *Change* 26(4): 10–20.

Means, Barbara, John Blando, Kerry Olson, Teresa Middleton, Catherine Cobb Morocco, Arlene R. Remz, and Judith Zorfass. 1993. *Using Technology to Support Educational Reform*. Washington, D.C: U.S. Department of Education, Office of Educational Research and Improvement. ED 364 220. 116pp. MF–01; PC–05.

Merchant, Betty. 1995. "Current Educational Reform: 'Shape-Shifting' or Genuine Improvement in the Quality of Teaching and Learning?" *Educational Theory* 45(2): 251–68.

Messick, S. 1984. "The Nature of Cognitive Styles: Problems and Promise in Educational Practice." *Educational Psychologist* 19(2): 59–74.

Miller, Roberta Balstad. 1995. "The Information Society: O Brave New World." *Social Science Computer Review* 13(2): 163–70.

Millet, J.D. 1962. *The Community of Scholars*. New York: Random House.

———. 1978. *New Structures of Campus Power*. San Francisco: Jossey-Bass.

Moncs-Hattal, B., et al. 1990. "Guidelines for Curricula in Computer Graphics in the Visual Arts." *Computer Graphics* 24(3): 78–113.

Moore, Michael G. 1989a. "Editorial: Three Types of Interaction." *American Journal of Distance Education* 3(2): 1–6.

———. 1989b. *Effects of Distance Learning: A Summary of the Literature*. Report prepared for the Office of Technology Assessment, Congress of the United States. Washington, D.C.: Government Printing Office.

Moore, Michael, and Melody M. Thompson, with B. Allan Quigley, G. Christopher Clark, and Gerald G. Goft. 1990. *The Effects of Distance Learning: A Summary of the Literature*. Research Monograph No. 2. University Park: Pennsylvania State University, American Center for the Study of Distance Education. ED 330 321. 83pp. MF–01; PC–04.

Muns, Raleigh C. 1995. "Online Scholarly Discussion Groups." In *Computer Mediated Communication and the Online Classroom., Volume I: Overview and Perspectives* edited by Zane L. Berge and Mauri P. Collins. Cresskill, N.J.: Hampton Press.

Murray, Alexander. 1978. *Reason and Society in the Middle Ages*. London: Oxford Univ. Press.

National Association of Scholars. 1996. *The Dissolution of General Education: 1914–1933*. Princeton, N.J.: Author.

National Center for Education Statistics [NCES]. 1995. *1995*

Educational Forecast. Washington, D.C.: U.S. Department of Education. Available: http://www.nces.edu

Nettles, Michael T. 1995. "The Emerging National Policy Agenda on Higher Education Assessment: A Wake-Up Call." *Review of Higher Education* 18(3): 293–313.

O'Banion, Terry. 1995–96. "A Learning College for the 21st Century." *Community College Journal* 66(3): 18–23.

Olcott, Donald J., Jr. 1992. "Policy Issues in Statewide Delivery of University Programs by Telecommunications." *American Journal of Distance Education* 6(2): 14–26.

Ostendorf, Virginia A. 1991. "Shopping for Satellite Curriculum." *Media & Methods* 27(November/December): 10.

Ouchi, W. 1981. *Theory Z: How American Businesses Can Meet the Japanese Challenges*. Reading, Mass.: Addison-Wesley.

Owens, R.G. 1987. *Organizational Behavior in Education*. 3d ed. Englewood Cliffs, N.J.: Prentice-Hall.

Parsons, T., and G.M. Platt. 1973. *The American University*. Cambridge, Mass.: Harvard Univ. Press.

Pascale, R.T., and A.G. Athos. 1981. *The Art of Japanese Management*. New York: Simon & Schuster.

Pascarella, Ernest T., and Patrick T. Terenzini. 1991. *How College Affects Students*. San Francisco: Jossey-Bass.

Paulsen, Michael B., and Kenneth A. Feldman. 1995. "Toward a Reconceptualization of Scholarship: A Human Action System with Functional Imperatives." *Journal of Higher Education* 66(6): 615–40.

Pennington, Hilary. 1994. "The Challenges and Opportunities of Workforce Development." *Leadership Abstracts* 7(7): 3–4. ED 371 796. 4pp. MF–01; PC–01.

Perelman, Lewis. 1992. *School's Out: A Radical New Formula for the Revitalization of America's Educational Systems*. New York: William Morrow.

Plater, William M. 1994. "Future Work: Faculty Time in the 21st Century." Keynote address to the Professional and Organizational Development Network in Higher Education, October 21, Portland, Oregon.

Price, Robert V., and Judi Repman. 1995. "Instructional Design for College-level Courses Using Interactive Television." *Journal of Educational Technology Systems* 23(3): 251–63.

Reed, Diane, and Thomas J. Sork. 1990. "Ethical Considerations in Distance Education." *American Journal of Distance Education* 4(2): 30–43.

Reilly, Kathleen P., and K.M. Gulliver. 1992. "Interstate

Authorization of Distance Higher Education via Telecommunications: The Developing National Consensus in Policy and Practice." *American Journal of Distance Education* 6(2): 3–16.

Rice, R. Eugene 1991. "The Academic Professor in Transition: Toward a New Social Function." *Teaching Sociology* 14: 12–23.

Rice, E. Eugene, and Lori Richlin. 1993. "Broadening the Concept of Scholarship in the Professions." In *Educating Professionals: Responding to New Expectations for Competence and Accountability,* edited by L. Curry, J.F. Wegin, and Associates. San Francisco: Jossey-Bass.

Richlin, Lori, ed. 1993. *Preparing Faculty for the New Conceptions of Scholarship.* New Directions for Teaching and Learning, No. 54. San Francisco: Jossey-Bass.

Riel, Margaret. 1994. "Educational Change in a Technology-Rich Environment." *Journal of Research on Computing in Education* 26(4): 452–74.

Roberts, Michael M. 1996. "Internet II: The Next Generation University Network." *Educom Review* 31(6): 1–2. Available: http://www.educom.edu/web/pubs/review/reviewArticles

Rockman, Saul. 1991. "Telecommunications and Restructuring: Supporting Change or Creating It." In *Education Policy and Telecommunications Technologies.* Washington, D.C.: U.S. Department of Education, Office of Educational Research and Improvement.

Romiszowski, Alex J. 1981. *Designing Instructional Systems: Decision Making in Course Planning and Curriculum Design.* New York: Nichols.

Royar, Robert. 1994. "New Horizons, Clouded Vistas." *Computers and Composition* 11(2): 93–105.

Rudolph, F. 1990. *The American College and University: A History.* Athens: Univ. of Georgia Press.

Russell, Thomas L. 1993. *The "No Significant Difference" Phenomenon As Reported in Research Reports, Summaries, and Papers.* Raleigh: North Carolina State Univ., Office of Instructional Telecommunications.

Saettler, P. 1968. *A History of Instructional Technology.* New York: McGraw-Hill.

———. 1990. *The Evolution of American Educational Technology.* Englewood, Colo.: Libraries Unlimited.

Santoro, Gerald M. 1995. "What Is Computer-Mediated Communication?" In *Computer Mediated Communications and the Online Classroom. Volume I: Overview and Perspectives,* edited by Zane L. Berge and Mauri P. Collins. Creskill, N.J.: Hampton Press.

Schlosser, Charles A., and Mary L. Anderson. 1994. *Distance Education: Review of the Literature*. Washington, D.C.: Association for Educational Communications and Technology.

Schon, Donald. 1995. "The New Scholarship Requires a New Epistemology." *Change* 27(6): 27–34.

Schrum, L. 1992. *Information Age Innovations: A Case Study of Online Professional Development*. ERIC Document Reproduction Service. ED346 849. 19pp. MF–01; PC–01.

Seels, Barbara B., and Rita C. Richey. 1994. *Instructional Technology: The Definition and Domains of the Field*. Washington, D.C.: Association for Educational Communications and Technology.

Senge, Peter M. 1990. *The Fifth Discipline: The Art and Practice of the Learning Organization*. New York: Doubleday Currency.

Seymour, Daniel T. 1992. *On Q: Causing Quality in Higher Education*. New York: ACE/Macmillan.

———. 1993. "Quality on Campus: Three Institutions, Three Beginnings." *Change* 25(3): 8–18.

Shale, Doug. 1988. "Toward a Reconceptualization of Distance Education." *American Journal of Distance Education* 2(3): 25–35.

Shapiro, Harold T. 1993. "Current Realities and Future Prospects." *Academe* 78(7): 10–16.

Shapiro, Wendy L., Katherine Roskos, and G. Phillip Cartwright. 1995. "Technology-Enhanced Learning Environments." *Change* 27(6): 67–69.

Sharon, Schlomo. 1984. *Cooperative Learning in the Classroom: Research in Desegregated Schools*. Hillsdale, N.J.: Lawrence Erlbaum Associates.

Sherr, Lawrence A., and Deborah J. Teeter, eds. 1991. *Total Quality Management in Higher Education*. New Directions in Institutional Research No. 71. San Francisco: Jossey-Bass.

Shils, Edward. 1978. "The Order of Learning in the United States from 1865 to 1920: The Ascendancy of the Universities." *Minerva* 16(2): 159–95.

Silberger, Katy. 1995. "The Higher Education Electronic Infrastructure: The Impact on Libraries and Computer Centers." In *Computer Mediated Communication and the Online Classroom. Volume I: Overview and Perspectives,* edited by Zane L. Berge and Mauri P. Collins. Creskill, N.J.: Hampton Press.

Simpson, William B. 1993. "Higher Education's Role in a New

Beginning." *Academe* 78(7): 17–19.

Slavin, Robert E. 1983. "When Does Cooperative Learning Increase Student Achievement?" *Psychological Bulletin* 94: 429–45.

———. 1985. *Cooperative Learning.* New York: Longman.

Sleeman, D., and J.S. Brown, eds. 1982. *Intelligent Tutoring Systems.* London: Academic Press.

"Slicing the Learning Pie: Stan Davis Interview." 1996. *Educom Review* 31(5): 1–4. Available: http://www.educom.edu/web/pubs/review/reviewArticles

Sloan, De Villo. 1994. "Total Quality Management in the Culture of Higher Education." *Review of Higher Education* 17(4): 447–64.

Smallen, David L. 1993. "Reengineering of Student Learning? A Second Opinion from Camelot." In *Reengineering Teaching and Learning in Higher Education: Sheltered Groves, Camelot, Windmills, and Malls,* edited by Robert C. Heterick, Jr. Professional Paper Series, # 10. Boulder, Colo.: CAUSE. ED 359 921. 57 pp. MF–01; PC–03.

Spaulding, C., and D. Lake. 1991. "Interactive Effects of Computer Network and Student Characteristics on Students' Writing and Collaboration." Paper presented at the annual meeting of the American Educational Research Association, April, Chicago, Illinois. ED 329 966. 26pp. MF–01; PC–02.

Sudweeks, Fay, Mauri Collins, and John December. 1995. "Internetwork Resources." In *Computer Mediated Communication and the Online Classroom. Volume I: Overview and Perspectives,* edited by Zane L. Berg and Mauri P. Collins. Cresskill, N.J.: Hampton Press.

Sutton, Don. 1996. "New Directions in Distance Learning." Paper presented at the American Federation of Teachers National Higher Education Issue Conference, March, San Francisco, California.

Taitt, Henry A. 1993. "Technology in the Classroom: Planning for Educational Change." *NASSP Curriculum Report* 22(4): 1–7.

Tannenbaum, Edward. 1971. *European Civilization Since the Middle Ages.* New York: John Wiley and Sons, Inc.

Tapscott, Don. 1995. *The Digital Economy: Promise and Peril in the Age of Networked Intelligence.* New York: McGraw-Hill.

Tapscott, Don, and Art Caston. 1993. *Paradigm Shift: The New Promise of Information Technology.* New York: McGraw-Hill.

Task Force on Technology in Higher Education. 1996. *Teaming Up with Technology: How Unions Can Harness the Technology Revolution on Campus.* Washington, D.C.: American Federation of Teachers.

Taylor, J.C. 1994. "Technology, Distance Education and the Tyranny of Proximity." *Higher Education Management* 6(2): 179–90.

Thompson, Ann D., Michael R. Simonson, and Constance P. Hargrave. 1992. *Educational Technology: A Review of the Literature.* Washington, D.C.: Association for Educational Communications and Technology.

Tomer, Christinger. 1992. "Emerging Electronic Library Services and the Idea of Location Independence." *Journal of Computing in Higher Education* 4(1): 88–121.

Toombs, William, and William G. Tierney 1991. Meeting the Mandate: *Renewing the College and Departmental Curriculum.* ASHE-ERIC Higher Education Report No. 6. Washington, D.C.: The George Washington University, School of Education and Human Development. ED 345 603. 124pp. MF–01; PC–05.

Tucker, Robert W. 1995a. "The Virtual Classroom: Quality and Assessment." *Syllabus* 9(1): 48–51.

———. 1995b. "Distance Learning Programs: Models and Alternatives." *Syllabus* 9(3): 42–46.

Turner, Judith Axel. 18 March 1987. "Software for Teaching Given Little Credit in Tenure Reviews. *Chronicle of Higher Education:* A1, A20.

Twigg, Carol A. 1993. "Information Technology–Enabling Transformation." In *Reengineering Teaching and Learning in Higher Education: Sheltered Groves, Camelot, Windmills, and Malls,* edited by Robert C. Heterick, Jr. Professional Paper Series #10. Boulder, Colo.: CAUSE. ED 359 921. 57 pp. MF–01; PC–03.

Tyler, R.W. 1975. "Have Educational Reforms since 1950 Created Quality Education?" *Viewpoints* 51(2): 35–57.

U.S. Congress, Office of Technology Assessment. 1989. *Linking for Learning: A New Course for Education.* (OTA-SET-430). Washington, D C.: Government Printing Office.

Veysey, L.R. 1970. *The Emergence of the American University.* Chicago: Univ. of Chicago Press.

Waggaman, John S. 1991. *Strategies and Consequences: Managing the Costs in Higher Education.* ASHE-ERIC Higher Education Report No. 8. Washington, D.C.: The George Washington University, School of Education and Human Development. ED 347 921. 148pp. MF–01; PC–06.

Wagner, Ellen D. 1990. "Looking at Distance Education Through an Education Technologist's Eyes." *American Journal of Distance Education* 4(1): 13–28.

West, Thomas W., and Stephen L. Daigle. 1993. "Comprehensive Universities: Refocusing for the Next Century." *In Reengineering*

Teaching and Learning in Higher Education: Sheltered Groves, Camelot, Windmills, and Malls, edited by Robert C. Heterick, Jr. Professional Paper Series, #10. Boulder, Colo.: CAUSE. ED 359 921. 57 pp. MF–01; PC–03.

Yavarkovsky, J. 1990. "A University Based Electronic Publishing Network." *Educom Review* 25: 14–20.

Zastrocky, Michael. 1995. "Strategic Planning for Technology." *Planning for Higher Education* 23(Spring): 59–60.

Zimmerman, W., and S. Cunningham, eds. 1991. *Visualization in Teaching and Learning Mathematics.* MAA Notes, Number 19. Washington, D.C.: Mathematical Association of America.

INDEX

A

battle of the snails, 47

Bell Laboratories, 75

Benditt, Theodore, 47

"beneficiaries," 77–78

Blau (1973) bifurcated model of higher education institutions, 72–73

Bleed (1993): community colleges defined excellence through
    service to many, 19–20

"blooming, buzzing organized anarchy," 91

Boise State University *The Electronic Renaissance*, 62

Bork (1991): agenda for empirical research studies on
    technology-based learning, 120

Boyer (1990), 47
    community college faculty perspective on student learning,
      121
    higher education focus shift to the building of a nation, 48
    proposes a four-dimensional model of scholarship, 55
    use a research model to evaluate and improve teaching, 59

Brigham (1994):
    measurement of success in early stages of TQM, 117
    "low key" approaches generate insufficient attention for
      implementing TQM, 77

Browser, 127

bureaucratic/academic institutions, 73

Bureaucratic Sphere reforming, 74–80

C

CAI. See Computer Assisted Instruction

California State University
    leveraging technologies to deal with enrollment growth, 2
    largest public comprehensive university system, 19

California State University-Chico distance learning
    opposed by a state higher education regulatory board, 96–97

Campus Computing survey
    of campuses supporting and rewarding faculty
      development of courseware, 117
    indicates instructional technology used at all types of higher
      education institutions, 122

Campus Trends 1995, 56

careful deliberation should not be confused with obfuscation, 104

Carnegie Foundation for the Advancement of Teaching, 55, 60, 66,
    85

Carnegie Commission on Higher Education institution kinds, 10

cascade model of implementing TQM, 77

Cross and Angelo (1988): research most likely to improve teaching and learning is in response to questions of users, 121

"a crossroads of information flow," 2

Crow (1994/95) on peer accreditation
good practices list in distance learning, 95
traditional standards should articulate with flexibility so not to squelch important innovation, 94

Crow and Rariden (1993):
introducing technology more complex than deploying it, 101

CSU. *See* California State University

Cuban (1986): cycle of failed attempts to integrate technological solutions to educational problems, 11

curriculum
as intentional design for learning negotiated by faculty, 41–42
intentional design for learning negotiated by faculty, 41–42

Curry (1992): problems in use of term profitability in TQM, 84

"customers," Seymour (1992) use of term, 77

CyberQ: a software assessment approach to adaptive assessment and quality management, 87

Cyberspace, 127

cycle of failed attempts to integrate technological solutions to educational problems, 11

D

Daly (1994): aggregative scholarship
as a bridge between scholarship and teaching, 53

Darby (1992): primary constraints neither technical nor pedagogical but organizational and social in nature, 11

database management systems
allows local distribution of accumulated information, 81

DBMS. See database management systems

Deal and Kennedy's *Corporate Cultures* (1982), 76

de emphasis of lectures, 3

delivery technologies divide into owned and leased, 105

Deming's "fourteen Points" for organizational leaders, 76–77

Demonstrations with computer animation techniques, 42

desktop groupware and video conferencing, 38

Detroit metropolitan area interactive technology , 107–108

DIALOG, 43

Direct Electronic Learning Teaching Alternative. See Project Delta

discussion greater potential than lectures, 35

Dissolution of General Education 1914-1993 (1996), 118

distanced interaction serves needs of traditional students, 2

distance education: recommend federal and private initiatives for
        sponsored research on, 120–121
distance learning
        accreditation guidelines for governing boards in, 96
        cannot necessarily be evaluated by standard measures
            applied to
        classroom education, 97
        critical technologies, 99–100
        good practices list for peer accreditation in, 95
        New constituencies appear well served by available
            venues, 116
        warning against abandoning traditional criteria in peer
            accreditation of, 94
distance learning students contact through on-ground education
        methods may be ineffective, 100
Distance learning theory, 24–25
"disturbing paradox" of higher education, 50, 50–51
doctoral dissertation role, 55–56
Dorris, Anna: *Visual Instruction in the Public School,* 3
Doucette (1993): entire higher education culture
        based upon the presumption of faculty prerogative, 60
Download, 127

E

early adopters benefit from jumping onto the instructional
        technology bandwagon, 124
East Carolina University use of instructional technologies, 2
Eastmond and Ziegahn's (1995): five stage design model, 26
education transformation from elite to mass to universal system, 50
"Educational Camelot," 1
        four-year liberal arts college as, 16
educational
        conservatives requirement, 9
        institutions need to become learning organizations, 68
        reform policies has two distinct perspectives, 9
        software and tenure decisions, 67–68
        technology funding determination, 91
        television development, 3
        use of information technology, 122
Education in Industry: major educational enterprises with little
        involvement of colleges and universities , 5
"electronic classrooms," 107
electronic databases as exploratory domain, 43

G

Geoghegan (1996): early adopters benefits from jumping onto the instructional technology bandwagon, 124

German influence caused paradigm shift with establishment of postgraduate studies, 50

German university research model, 49

Gilbert (1996): on inertia in our higher education system, 119,122

Glavin, President William F., 81

Goldstein (1991): warns against abandoning traditional criteria in peer accreditation, 94

good practices list for peer accreditation in distance learning, 95

good teaching in postsecondary education recognition, 60

Gopher, 127

graduate engineering programs use of satellites to deliver, 110

Gross (1995): known for years that Instruction Paradigm is not best way to teach, 14

Gross, Muscarella, and Pirkl (1994): divide delivery technologies into owned and leased, 105

Gunawardena (1990): information technology providing capability of serving a much larger audience, 102

Gunawardena (1994): definition of learner-interface interaction, 41

H

Hahn and Jackson (1995):
  careful deliberation should not be confused with obfuscation, 104
  information technology doesnÕt necessarily save, 102
  problems determining type of educational technology to fund, 91

Hamilton College as "educational Camelot," 1

Harnad (1990): Internet and World Wide Web promise to substantially restructure the pursuit of knowledge, 60

Harvard College, 47

Hatch Act of 1887, 48

Hau use of TQM in teaching business statistics, 86

Hayes (1990): adult educators as facilitators should involve adult learners in a collaborative process, 28

Hendrickson and Bartkovich (1986): enhanced bifurcated model of higher education institutions, 72

Heterick (1993): opportunity and technology to break with traditional higher education paradigm, 9

Hewlett-Packard invites California State University-Chico to deliver credit classes, 96–97

Hezel and Dirr (1991): older non traditional students prevented from attending traditional classes due to responsibilities, 34 higher education

    historically one of severest criticisms of, 33

    model based upon the needs of the global marketplace
        proposed by Nemorowicz and Rosi, 87

    primary need of, 8

    requiring efforts to define academic productivity, 115–116

Homepage, 127

Host, 127

HotBot, 128

HTML. See Hypertext Mark-up Language

Humboldt, Wilhelm von, 49

Hypertext, 127

Hypertext Mark-up Language, 127

Hypertext Supreme Court Cases of Cornell University, 62

I

idea champions should identify and encourage, 103

ideal learning environment has two characteristics, 15

Illinois State Board of Education rejection of "instructional format"
    of distance learning, 97

improving

    the administrative system, 79–80

    work performance by implementing the PDCA cycle, 78–79

"inadvertent Trojan Horse" of Sloan (1994), 87

"independent entrepreneurs"

  faculty consider themselves as, 84–85

inertia within our higher education system, 119

infection model of implementing TQM, 77

information and communication technologies as "magic bullet, " 8

Information clearinghouses for courseware, 61–62

Information Resource Management role, 80–83

information technology

    does not necessarily save time or money, 102

    providing a capability of serving a much larger audience, 102

infrastructure investment decisions require global perspective, 99

input assessment of quality in undergraduate education, 7

Institutional changes carries significant political implications, 9

institutional governing board

    advocates as well as guardians of long-term best interests, 98

    mechanisms for creating learning opportunities, 98–99

institutionalization, 10–11

institutional variables as critical element

    in defining faculty roles and responsibilities, 21

institutions

    moving toward research and away from teaching and
       service, 56

    should focus on specific users, 100

instruction, programmed and auto-tutorial, 3

instructional design, 25

    variables that need to be incorporated into process, 26–27

"instructional epiphany," 124

instructional technologies applications, 1

    need for academic support for creation of, 118

instructional technology leadership from teachers, 24

Instructional Television Fixed Service, 93

Instruction Paradigm, 14

instruction versus learning paradigms, 14–15

integrated database would permit the creation of a virtual folder for
    each student, 82

Integrated Services Digital Networks, 93, 128

integrative nature of change within an organization, 10

Intelligent CAI, 3, 43

Intelligent Tutoring Systems. *See* Intelligent CAI

interdisciplinary initiatives result of scholarship of integration, 57

InterEd, Inc.'s CyberQ as a software assessment approach to
    adaptive assessment and quality management, 87

Interface Capabilities, 41–42

internal dialogue, 34

Internet, 127

    made possible a collapse of the historic barriers between
       faculty and other units, 64

    as backbone for today's online scholarly communication
       and collaboration, 60

Internet and World Wide Web

  promise to substantially restructure the pursuit of knowledge, 60

Internet listservers as distribution mechanism, 64

interpretation as part of scholarship of integration, 57

IRM. See Information Resource Management

ISDN. See Integrated Services Digital Networks

issues needing solving before implementation of a paradigmatic
    shift, 15

ITFS. *See* Instructional Television Fixed Service

ITS. *See* Intelligent Tutoring Systems

J

Japanese management techniques using TQM principles, 74–75

Jaspers, Griffith and Wagener:
  research as part of the definition of a university, 53
Jauch (1976): survey of natural science faculty demonstrate belief
  that research increases classroom effectiveness, 53
John Hopkins University founding as the most decisive single event
  in the history of learning in the Western hemisphere, 50
Johnstone (1990):
  pioneering efforts on finessing ways through labyrinth of
    state rules and regulations, 96
  questions on regulatory responsibility, 92
Jones Intercable, 2

K

Kaizen. See Total Quality Management
Kearsley and Lynch (1992): much instructional technology leader-
  ship comes from teachers encouraging its use, 24
Keig and Waggoner (1994)
  professional development consultants expertise outside of
    counseled disciplines produces cultural resistance, 24
KN. *See* Knowledge Network
Knowledge Network as true "virtual university," 2
Knowles (1984):
  adult educators need to function more as facilitators than
    content experts, 28
  adults possess six characteristics distinct from younger
    learners, 27–28

L

leadership not the same as management, especially in professional
  organizations, 102
"leading technologies" three-part typology especially useful, 105
learner-content interaction as hallmark of education, 34
learner-instructor interaction dominant mode, 34
learner-interface interaction, 41
learner-learner
  classroom interaction, 35–36
  interaction in the virtual classroom, 40
learner's self-concept as possessed by adult learners, 27
learning environments as communications technologies, 42
learning organizations are what educational institutions need be, 68
Learning Paradigm
  focus shift from providing instruction to producing
    learning, 14

possible by empowering students to determine the
venue, 33
learning styles as types of behavior, 23
learning styles of students, 22–23
lecture format philosophic support, 34
liberal arts exposure value for students, 119
Library of Congress has nearly 25 terabytes of data in holdings, 63
library staffing and funding
should retain a strong commitment to adequate, 123–124
Linking for Learning
Office of Technology Assessment suggests analyzing eight
elements that affect overall costs, 105
Listserv, 128
Locke, John: *An Essay Concerning Human Understanding*, 34
loose-tight model of implementing TQM, 77
"low key" approaches risk generating insufficient attention for
implementing TQM, 77
Lusterman on Education in Industry, 5
Lycos, 128
Lynton (1984):
higher education continues to face a "disturbing
paradox," 50

M

McClure (1993): colleges and universities are communities of
scholars, 72, 74
"magic bullet" for reducing costs while simultaneously improving
instruction via information and communication technologics, 8
Mailing list server. See Listserv
Management by Objectives, 116
Marchese (1993): began in the eighties but big wave of interest
kicked in during the 1991-92 academic year, 75
Maricopa County Community College District
budget to keep computing infrastructure current of, 107
Mario Andretti school of change, 9
Markwood and Johnstone: costs warranted if extend access and
enable success of underserved student populations, 103
Martin and Samels (1995):
importance of understanding potential of electronic
infrastructure for distance learning, 98
institutions should focus on specific users rather than all
possible users, 100
Mastery Learning, 3

matching or mismatching student learning styles, 23

measuring competence of students rather than "seat time," 87

measuring evidence of quality in undergraduate education, 7–8

media comparison review of several decades of studies, 38–39

Merchant (1995): issues needing solving before implementation of a paradigmatic shift, 15

MFJ. See Modification of Final Judgment

microworlds as exploratory domain, 43, 44

Miller (1995): moving of institutions toward research and away from teaching and service, 56

Millet (1962): colleges and universities are communities of scholars, 72

Millet (1978):

    collegial model of higher education has limitations, 72

    "community of scholars" organizational type, 74

Mind Extension University. See Knowledge Network

mission statement as ethos of an institution, 10

MIT

    junior faculty member in civil engineering denied tenure because research could not be evaluated, 66–67

    Project Athena in 1982 to study the use of computers in undergraduate education, 67–68

Moberly, Sir Walter: believed University should not engage in research, 53

Modem, 128

Modification of Final Judgment

    broke Bell System into regional components, 92

monograph, organization of this, 12

Moore and Thompson (1990):

    four variables need to be incorporated into the instructional design process, 26–27

    recommend federal and private initiatives for sponsored research

    on distance education, 120–121

"Moore's Law," 1

Morrill Act of 1862, 48

motivation as possessed by adult learners, 28

Mount Everest mentality in electronic technologies, xi

Multimedia Textbooks of Virtual Hospital at University of Iowa, 62

Muns (1995): contends using network requires no more time or intellect than learning to play ordinary card or board games, 64

Murrow referring to the early potential of radio, 13

N

O

Q

quality needs valid reliable measures, 8, 77-78
quality standards for certificate and degree programs need, 121–122
Queens University SunSITE, 61

R

RBOCs. See Regional Bell Operating Companies
readiness to learn as possessed by adult learners, 27–28
reform as a condition where direction of change are known, 10
regulation of intra- and interstate delivery systems issues, 96
regulatory
> issues need to be addressed by governing boards, 91–98
> responsibility questions, 92

Reilly and Gulliver (1992): evaluation of distance learning, 97
relative advantage as factor influencing faculty adoption, 22
research enhances teaching belief, 53
research model used to evaluate and improve teaching, 59
restructuring scholarly activity to include great teaching reaffirms
> teaching centrality at research institutions, 59–60

review of extended case studies of institutional experimentation
> with TQM in higher education, 86

Rice (1991): need fresh dialogue on scholarship of teaching, 60
Rockman's (1991) "technohype," 11
Rogers emphasis on student in higher education, 13–14
Role and Nature of the Doctoral Dissertation, 55
role of the learner's experience as possessed by adult learners, 27
"rules of the game" as organizational culture, 77
Russell (1983): review of decades of media comparison studies,
> 38–39

S

"sage on the stage," 114–115
Saint Augustine College Project Gutenberg, 43
Saint Louis University
> instructional technologies to enhance traditional programs, 2

Satellite Delivery, 99, 108–110
Schlosser and Anderson (1994): requirements for higher education
> voice in federal communications policy, 94

scholarly achievement not a high priority in early U.S. colleges, 47
scholarly skywriting, 63–64
scholarship and teaching, 52–53
scholarship of application, 57–59
scholarship of discovery, 55–57

consolidates graduate training with the research function, 55

empiricism is prevailing institutional epistemology of, 65

on doorstep of a major revolution, 62

scholarship of integration, 57

scholarship of teaching, 59–60

  can't be any such thing as, 67

  suggestion should have a fresh dialogue on, 60

Scholarship Reconsidered proposes a four-dimensional model, 55

scholarship reconceptualization, 51–60

Schon (1985): "technical rationality," 65

Schon (1995):

    battle of the snails, 47

    can't be any such thing as scholarship of teaching, 67

    new forms of scholarship must be testably valid, 66

    Project Athena purpose, 67–68

Scottish model of regularized curriculum, 49

Search Engine, 128

self-pacing, 3

Senge (1990): successful corporations are already becoming become learning organizations, 68

Server, 128

service added to the mission of private and public universities with passage of the Morrill Act of 1862, 48

service must be distinguished from citizenship, 58

Seymour (1992) use of term "customers," 77

Seymour (1993): three common approaches to implementing TQM, 77

Shale (1988): defining characteristic of education, 39–40

Shapiro, Roskos and Cartwright (1995): distinguishing between different video teleconferencing systems, 107

Shareware, 128

Sherr and Teeter (1991): review of higher education extended case studies of TQM institutional experimentation, 86

"Shewhart cycle." *See* "the PDCA cycle"

Shewhart statistical quality control method, 75

Shils (1978): John Hopkins University founding as most decisive single event in history of learning in Western hemisphere, 50

Silberger (1995): scholarly skywriting, 63–64

Simpson (1993): value of a liberal arts exposure before vocational emphasis or professional specialization, 119

Sloan (1994): teaching TQM as academic subject

  causes it to be an "inadvertent Trojan Horse," 87

Smallen (1993):

two characteristics of ideal learning environment, 15
"variances from the ideal," 1
smart lectern teaching station, 107
social science research should benefit from new information
   technologies, 63
software assessment approach to adaptive assessment and quality
   management, 87
specialist as a replacement for the professor, 15
standard accounting in higher education, 74–75
Stanford University
   Computer Assisted Instruction at, 43
   electronic versions of technology transfer offices of, 65
State Higher Education Executive Officers, 96
state regulations
   for instructional telecommunications programs, 96–98
   pioneering efforts on finessing ways through labyrinth of, 96
Strategic Planning for Technology, 98–104
students for life, certified graduates as, 6
successful application of technology to the learning process
   will address variances from the ideal learning environment, 16
SunSITE, 61
Suppes Computer Assisted Instruction at Stanford, 43
support for faculty required when many attempt to use new
   instructional technology, 125
support structures required for success, 124–125
Surf, 128
survey demonstrates that research increases classroom
   effectiveness, 53
Synchronous, 128
system of tenure and promotion necessitates fairly rigid timetables
   for launching research projects and publishing results, 56
system thinking effect on curriculum and course design , 3

T

Tapscott (1996): organizational learning is only substantial
   competitive advantage, 71
Tapscott and Caston (1993): lack of "comprehensive
   implementation" of the new IRM model, 81
Task Force on Technology in Higher Education
   condemn ad hoc decision-making in technology
      procurement, 120
taxonomy of
   colleges and universities that accommodates political

Theory Z, 76

TLTR. See Teaching, Learning, and Technology Roundtables

Tomer (1992): speculates that full-text libraries will be converted
into machine-readable format and made available for
FTP, 63

Toombs and Tierney (1991)

definition of reform of, 10

propose identifying and encouraging idea champions, 103

Total Quality Management, 75

as meeting or exceeding customer needs, 75

concepts should that encourages dialogue, 88

implementation should begin on the service side, 83

issues that need to address before can implement, 117

measurement of success in early stages of, 117

philosophy emphasizing continuous improvement, 76, 80

success requires permeate higher education culture , 77

three common approaches to implementing, 77

where works in Academic setting, 117

TQM. *See* Total Quality Management

Traditional Classroom

structural components and unrealized potential, 33–36

transmuted into "a crossroads of information flow," 2

traditional faculty development examples, 21

traditional higher education paradigm

opportunity and technology to break with, 9

traditionalists against technology enthusiasts, 122–123

trialability as factor that influences faculty adoption, 22

Tucker (1995): organizes communication technologies between the
instructor and students as well as among students, 105

Tucker (1995b)

distance learning students contact through on-ground
education

methods may be ineffective, 100

soon there will be territorial disputes as distance learning
providers exploit the global market, 97–98

suggests advantage to asynchronous interaction, 40

Snapshots of a Movement, 86

two-way audio classrooms, 37-38

"tyranny of proximity," 45

U

"unit mastery," 3

Universal Resource Locator, 128

universities focus for discovery and diffusion of knowledge, 48-49
university research as part of its definition, 53
University of Chicago foundation, 50
University of Iowa *Multimedia Textbooks* of Virtual Hospital, 62
University of Pennsylvania *The Virtual Media Lab*, 62
University of Texas World Lecture Hall, 61–62
University of Wisconsin use TQM in teaching business statistics, 86
URL. See Universal Resource Locator
Usenet newsgroups as distribution mechanism, 64
users of the system identification important, 100

V
validation as defining characteristic of education, 40
"variances from the ideal"
 introduction of targeted applications to address, 1
Video Teleconferencing, 99–100
 distinguish between different systems of, 107
 illustration of costs associated with using, 107–108
Virginia Community College System, 110
virtual, xi
virtual campus
 as a metaphor, 1
 potential for interaction, 39–41
 types of interaction, 39
Virtual Classroom, 36–39
 as more scrutable environments for objective, automated
  assessment, 86–87
Virtual Hospital, 62
Virtual Media Lab from the University of Pennsylvania, 62
visual instructional materials
 calls for the integration into the curriculum of, 3
Visual Instruction in the Public School, 3

W
Wayne County Community College, xi
 costs associated with video teleconferencing at, 107–108
WCCC. *See* Wayne County Community College
Web/Web Site, 129
Western Cooperative for Educational Telecommunications, 87, 121
Western Governors Association
 measuring competence of students rather than "seat time,"
  87
Western Governors University, 2

built quality measures into its very structure, 87
Western Interstate Commission for Higher Education, 121
Western Michigan University
emphasize on business education users, 100
WGA. *See* Western Governors Association
WGU. *See* Western Governors University
WICHE. *See* Western Interstate Commission for Higher Education
work and learning synonymous in today's information economy, 71
The World Lecture Hall at the University of Texas, 61–62
World Wide Web, 129
homepages constructed for sole purpose of brokering
information on curriculum development, 61
most popular Internet network, 60
WWW. *See* World Wide Web

Y

Yavarkovsky (1990) use of phrase "the collaboratory," 64
Yuppie toy approach, xi

Z

Zastrocky (1995) use of new technology to become more efficient
in performing ineffective operations, 102
Zero-Based Budgeting, 116

ASHE-ERIC HIGHER EDUCATION REPORTS

Since 1983, the Association for the Study of Higher Education (ASHE) and the Educational Resources Information Center (ERIC) Clearinghouse on Higher Education, a sponsored project of the Graduate School of Education and Human Development at The George Washington University, have cosponsored the ASHE-ERIC Higher Education Report series. This volume is the twenty-fifth overall and the eighth to be published by the Graduate School of Education and Human Development at The George Washington University.

Each monograph is the definitive analysis of a tough higher education problem, based on thorough research of pertinent literature and institutional experiences. Topics are identified by a national survey. Noted practitioners and scholars are then commissioned to write the reports, with experts providing critical reviews of each manuscript before publication.

Eight monographs (10 before 1985) in the ASHE-ERIC Higher Education Report series are published each year and are available on individual and subscription bases. To order, use the order form on the last page of this book.

Qualified persons interested in writing a monograph for the ASHE-ERIC Higher Education Report series are invited to submit a proposal to the National Advisory Board. As the preeminent literature review and issue analysis series in higher education, the Higher Education Reports are guaranteed wide dissemination and national exposure for accepted candidates. Execution of a monograph requires at least a minimal familiarity with the ERIC database, including *Resources in Education* and the current *Index to Journals in Education*. The objective of these reports is to bridge conventional wisdom with practical research. Prospective authors are strongly encouraged to call Dr. Fife at 800/773-3742.

For further information, write to
    ASHE-ERIC Higher Education Reports
    The George Washington University
    One Dupont Circle, Suite 630
    Washington, DC 20036
Or phone (202) 296-2597; toll free: 800-773-ERIC.

Write or call for a complete catalog.

Visit our Web site at www.gwu.edu/~eriche

ADVISORY BOARD

James Earl Davis
University of Delaware at Newark

Cassie Freeman
Peabody College–Vanderbilt University

Susan Frost
Emory University

Mildred Garcia
Arizona State University West

James Hearn
University of Georgia

Philo Hutcheson
Georgia State University

CONSULTING EDITORS

Thomas A. Angelo
AAHE Assessment Forum

Sandra Beyer
University of Texas at El Paso

Robert Boice
State University of New York–Stony Brook

Steve Brigham
American Association for Higher Education

Ivy E. Broder
The American University

Robert A. Cornesky
Cornesky and Associates, Inc.

Barbara Gross Davis
University of California at Berkeley

James R. Davis
Center for Academic Quality and Assessment of Student
    Learning

Cheryl Falk
Yakima Valley Community College

L. Dee Fink
University of Oklahoma

Anne H. Frank
American Association of University Professors

Joseph E. Gilmore
Northwest Missouri State University

Kenneth C. Green
Claremont Graduate School

Dean L. Hubbard
Northwest Missouri State University

Mardee Jenrette
Miami-Dade Community College

Clara M. Lovett
Northern Arizona University

Howard T. Major
Grand Valley State University

Laurence R. Marcus
Rowan College

Robert Menges
Northwestern University

Diane E. Morrison
Centre for Curriculum and Professional Development

L. Jackson Newell
University of Utah

Steven G. Olswang
University of Washington

Brent Ruben
State University of New Jersey–Rutgers

Steven G. Sachs
Northern Virginia Community College

Sherry Sayles-Folks
Eastern Michigan University

Daniel Seymour
Claremont College–California

Pamela D. Sherer
The Center for Teaching Excellence

Marilla D. Svinicki
University of Texas–Austin

David Sweet
OERI, U.S. Department of Education

Gershon Vincow
Syracuse University

W. Allan Wright
Dalhousie University

Donald H. Wulff
University of Washington

Manta Yorke
Liverpool John Moores University

REVIEW PANEL

Charles Adams
University of Massachusetts–Amherst

Louis Albert
American Association for Higher Education

Richard Alfred
University of Michigan

Henry Lee Allen
University of Rochester

Philip G. Altbach
Boston College

Marilyn J. Amey
University of Kansas

Kristine L. Anderson
Florida Atlantic University

Karen D. Arnold
Boston College

Robert J. Barak
Iowa State Board of Regents

Alan Bayer
Virginia Polytechnic Institute and State University

John P. Bean
Indiana University–Bloomington

John M. Braxton
Peabody College, Vanderbilt University

Ellen M. Brier
Tennessee State University

Barbara E. Brittingham
The University of Rhode Island

Dennis Brown
University of Kansas

Peter McE. Buchanan
Council for Advancement and Support of Education

Patricia Carter
University of Michigan

John A. Centra
Syracuse University

Arthur W. Chickering
George Mason University

Darrel A. Clowes
Virginia Polytechnic Institute and State University

Cynthia S. Dickens
Mississippi State University

Deborah M. DiCroce
Piedmont Virginia Community College

Sarah M. Dinham
University of Arizona

Kenneth A. Feldman
State University of New York–Stony Brook

Dorothy E. Finnegan
The College of William & Mary

Mildred Garcia
Montclair State College

Rodolfo Z. Garcia
Commission on Institutions of Higher Education

Kenneth C. Green
University of Southern California

James Hearn
University of Georgia

Edward R. Hines
Illinois State University

Deborah Hunter
University of Vermont

Philo Hutcheson
Georgia State University

Bruce Anthony Jones
University of Pittsburgh

Elizabeth A. Jones
The Pennsylvania State University

Kathryn Kretschmer
University of Kansas

Marsha V. Krotseng
State College and University Systems of West Virginia

George D. Kuh
Indiana University–Bloomington

Daniel T. Layzell
University of Wisconsin System

Patrick G. Love
Kent State University

Cheryl D. Lovell
State Higher Education Executive Officers

Meredith Jane Ludwig
American Association of State Colleges and Universities

Dewayne Matthews
Western Interstate Commission for Higher Education

Mantha V. Mehallis
Florida Atlantic University

Toby Milton
Essex Community College

James R. Mingle
State Higher Education Executive Officers

John A. Muffo
Virginia Polytechnic Institute and State University

L. Jackson Newell
Deep Springs College

James C. Palmer
Illinois State University

Robert A. Rhoads
The Pennsylvania State University

G. Jeremiah Ryan
Harford Community College

Mary Ann Danowitz Sagaria
The Ohio State University

Daryl G. Smith
The Claremont Graduate School

William G. Tierney
University of Southern California

Susan B. Twombly
University of Kansas

Robert A. Walhaus
University of Illinois–Chicago

Harold Wechsler
University of Rochester

Elizabeth J. Whitt
University of Illinois–Chicago

Michael J. Worth
The George Washington University

RECENT TITLES

Volume 25 ASHE-ERIC Higher Education Reports

1. A Culture for Academic Excellence: Implementing the Quality Principles in Higher Education
   Jann E. Freed, Marie R. Klugman, and Jonathan D. Fife

2. From Discipline to Development: Rethinking Student Conduct in Higher Education
   Michael Dannells

3. Academic Controversy: Enriching College Instruction Through Intellectual Conflict
   David W. Johnson, Roger T. Johnson, and Karl A. Smith

4. Higher Education Leadership: Analyzing the Gender Gap
   Luba Chliwniak

Volume 24 ASHE-ERIC Higher Education Reports

1. Tenure, Promotion, and Reappointment: Legal and Administrative Implications (951)
   Benjamin Baez and John A. Centra

2. Taking Teaching Seriously: Meeting the Challenge of Instructional Improvement (952)
   Michael B. Paulsen and Kenneth A. Feldman

3. Empowering the Faculty: Mentoring Redirected and Renewed (953)
   Gaye Luna and Deborah L. Cullen

4. Enhancing Student Learning: Intellectual, Social, and Emotional Integration (954)
   Anne Goodsell Love and Patrick G. Love

5. Benchmarking in Higher Education: Adapting Best Practices to Improve Quality (955)
   Jeffrey W. Alstete

6. Models for Improving College Teaching: A Faculty Resource (956)
   Jon E. Travis

7. Experiential Learning in Higher Education: Linking Classroom and Community (957)
   Jeffrey A. Cantor

8. Successful Faculty Development and Evaluation: The Complete Teaching Portfolio (958)
   John P. Murray

Volume 23 ASHE-ERIC Higher Education Reports

1. The Advisory Committee Advantage: Creating an Effective Strategy for Programmatic Improvement (941)
   Lee Teitel

2. Collaborative Peer Review: The Role of Faculty in Improving College Teaching (942)
   Larry Keig and Michael D. Waggoner

8. Turning Teaching into Learning: The Role of Student Responsibility in the Collegiate Experience (938)
   Todd M. Davis and Patricia Hillman Murrell

Volume 21 ASHE-ERIC Higher Education Reports

1. The Leadership Compass: Values and Ethics in Higher Education (921)
   John R. Wilcox and Susan L. Ebbs

2. Preparing for a Global Community: Achieving an International Perspective in Higher Education (922)
   Sarah M. Pickert

3. Quality: Transforming Postsecondary Education (923)
   Ellen Earle Chaffee and Lawrence A. Sherr

4. Faculty Job Satisfaction: Women and Minorities in Peril (924)
   Martha Wingard Tack and Carol Logan Patitu

5. Reconciling Rights and Responsibilities of Colleges and Students: Offensive Speech, Assembly, Drug Testing, and Safety (925)
   Annette Gibbs

6. Creating Distinctiveness: Lessons from Uncommon Colleges and Universities (926)
   Barbara K. Townsend, L. Jackson Newell, and Michael D. Wiese

7. Instituting Enduring Innovations: Achieving Continuity of Change in Higher Education (927)
   Barbara K. Curry

8. Crossing Pedagogical Oceans: International Teaching Assistants in U.S. Undergraduate Education (928)
   Rosslyn M. Smith, Patricia Byrd, Gayle L. Nelson, Ralph Pat Barrett, and Janet C. Constantinides

Quantity   **Amount**

_____ Please begin my subscription to the current year's
ASHE-ERIC Higher Education Reports (Volume 25) at
$120.00, over 33% off the cover price, starting with
Report 1.   _____

_____ Please send a complete set of Volume ____ *ASHE-ERIC*
Higher Education Reports at $120.00, over 33% off the
cover price.   _____

Individual reports are available for $24.00 and include the cost of shipping and handling.

SHIPPING POLICY:

- Books are sent UPS Ground or equivalent. For faster delivery, call for charges.
- Alaska, Hawaii, U.S. Territories, and Foreign Countries, please call for shipping information.
- Order will be shipped within 24 hours after receipt of request.
- Orders of 10 or more books, call for shipping information.

All prices shown are subject to change.

Returns: No cash refunds—credit will be applied to future orders.

PLEASE SEND ME THE FOLLOWING REPORTS:

Quantity	Volume/No.	Title	Amount

Please check one of the following: **Subtotal:** _____
☐ Check enclosed, payable to GWU-ERIC.
☐ Purchase order attached.   **Less Discount:** _____
☐ Charge my credit card indicated below:
   ☐ Visa   ☐ MasterCard   **Total Due:** _____

Expiration Date_____

Name_____

Title_____

Institution _____

Address_____

City _____ State _____ Zip_____

Phone _____ Fax _____ Telex_____

Signature _____ Date_____

SEND ALL ORDERS TO: ASHE-ERIC Higher Education Reports
The George Washington University
One Dupont Cir., Ste. 630, Washington, DC 20036-1183
Phone: (202) 296-2597 • Toll-free: 800/773-ERIC
FAX: (202) 452-1844
www.gwu.edu/~eriche